Macmillan Computer Science Series
Consulting Editor
Professor F.H. Sumner, University of Mancheste

S.T. Allworth and R.N. Zobel, *Introduction to*
second edition
Ian O. Angell and Gareth Griffith, *High-resolution Computer Graphics Using*
FORTRAN 77
Ian O. Angell and Gareth Griffith, *High-resolution Computer Graphics Using*
Pascal
M. Azmoodeh, *Abstract Data Types and Algorithms*
C. Bamford and P. Curran, *Data Structures, Files and Databases*
Philip Barker, *Author Languages for CAL*
A.N. Barrett and A.L. Mackay, *Spatial Structure and the Microcomputer*
R.E. Berry, B.A.E. Meekings and M.D. Soren, *A Book on C, second edition*
G.M. Birtwistle, *Discrete Event Modelling on Simula*
B.G. Blundell, C.N. Daskalakis, N.A.E. Heyes and T.P. Hopkins, *An*
Introductory Guide to Silvar Lisco and HILO Simulators
T.B. Boffey, *Graph Theory in Operations Research*
Richard Bornat, *Understanding and Writing Compilers*
Linda E.M. Brackenbury, *Design of VLSI Systems — A Practical Introduction*
J.K. Buckle, *Software Configuration Management*
W.D. Burnham and A.R. Hall, *Prolog Programming and Applications*
J.C. Cluley, *Interfacing to Microprocessors*
J.C. Cluley, *Introduction to Low Level Programming for Microprocessors*
Robert Cole, *Computer Communications, second edition*
Derek Coleman, *A Structured Programming Approach to Data*
Andrew J.T. Colin, *Fundamentals of Computer Science*
Andrew J.T. Colin, *Programming and Problem-solving in Algol 68*
S.M. Deen, *Fundamentals of Data Base Systems*
S.M. Deen, *Principles and Practice of Database Systems*
Tim Denvir, *Introduction to Discrete Mathematics for Software Engineering*
P.M. Dew and K.R. James, *Introduction to Numerical Computation in Pascal*
M.R.M. Dunsmuir and G.J. Davies, *Programming the UNIX System*
D. England *et al., A Sun User's Guide*
K.C.E. Gee, *Introduction to Local Area Computer Networks*
J.B. Gosling, *Design of Arithmetic Units for Digital Computers*
M.G. Hartley, M. Healey and P.G. Depledge, *Mini and Microcomputer Systems*
Roger Hutty, *Z80 Assembly Language Programming for Students*
Roland N. Ibbett, *The Architecture of High Performance Computers*
Patrick Jaulent, *The 68000 — Hardware and Software*
P. Jaulent, L. Baticle and P. Pillot, *68020–30 Microprocessors and their*
Coprocessors
J.M. King and J.P. Pardoe, *Program Design Using JSP — A Practical*
Introduction
H. Kopetz, *Software Reliability*
E.V. Krishnamurthy, *Introductory Theory of Computer Science*
V.P. Lane, *Security of Computer Based Information Systems*
Graham Lee, *From Hardware to Software — an introduction to computers*
A.M. Lister, *Fundamentals of Operating Systems, third edition*
G.P. McKeown and V.J. Rayward-Smith, *Mathematics for Computing*

(continued overleaf)

Brian Meek, *Fortran, PL/1 and the Algols*
A. Mével and T. Guéguen, *Smalltalk-80*
Barry Morrell and Peter Whittle, *CP/M 80 Programmer's Guide*
Derrick Morris, *System Programming Based on the PDP11*
Y. Nishinuma and R. Espesser, *UNIX — First contact*
Pim Oets, *MS-DOS and PC-DOS — A Practical Guide*
Christian Queinnec, *LISP*
E.J. Redfern, *Introduction to Pascal for Computational Mathematics*
Gordon Reece, *Microcomputer Modelling by Finite Differences*
W.P. Salman, O. Tisserand and B. Toulout, *FORTH*
L.E. Scales, *Introduction to Non-linear Optimization*
Peter S. Sell, *Expert Systems — A Practical Introduction*
Colin J. Theaker and Graham R. Brookes, *A Practical Course on Operating Systems*
M.R. Tolhurst *et al.*, *Open Systems Interconnection*
J.-M. Trio, *8086–8088 Architecture and Programming*
M.J. Usher, *Information Theory for Information Technologists*
B.S. Walker, *Understanding Microprocessors*
Peter J.L. Wallis, *Portable Programming*
Colin Walls, *Programming Dedicated Microprocessors*
I.R. Wilson and A.M. Addyman, *A Practical Introduction to Pascal—with BS6192, second edition*

Non-series
Roy Anderson, *Management, Information Systems and Computers*
I.O. Angell, *Advanced Graphics with the IBM Personal Computer*
J.E. Bingham and G.W.P. Davies, *A Handbook of Systems Analysis, second edition*
J.E. Bingham and G.W.P. Davies, *Planning for Data Communications*
B.V. Cordingley and D. Chamund, *Advanced BASIC Scientific Subroutines*
N. Frude, *A Guide to SPSS/PC+*

Open Systems Interconnection

Peter Boait
Geoff Neville
Ruth Norris
Michael Pickman
Mark Tolhurst (Editor)
John Walmsley

MACMILLAN
EDUCATION

First published 1988

Published by
MACMILLAN EDUCATION LTD
Houndmills, Basingstoke, Hampshire RG21 2XS
and London
Companies and representatives
throughout the world

Printed in Hong Kong

British Library Cataloguing in Publication Data
Open systems interconnection.—(Macmillan
   computer science series).
   1. Open computer systems
   I. Boait, Peter   II. Tolhurst, Mark
   004.6′2

   ISBN 0-333-46803-1

Contents

List of Figures

Preface

Information is increasingly recognised as a commodity whose value rises in proportion to its portability. From financial institutions operating in markets across the world to car makers running automated production lines, many businesses depend upon the immediate and reliable transfer of information from one computer system to another.

In a market-place bedevilled by the incompatibility of so many of the products on sale, this apparently straightforward requirement has proved extremely difficult to satisfy. Although individual manufacturers have provided proprietary solutions, these have not proved adequate to achieve the ultimate goal — full compatibility in communication between computer systems.

In common with similar moves in other areas of information technology, the International Organization for Standardization (ISO) has therefore overseen the production of a model for *open systems interconnection* (OSI) — that is, the facility for one OSI-compliant system to be able to interact with any other OSI-compliant system. The intention is that the OSI model and its associated standards will be universally accepted as the framework for the future development of inter-system communications.

From the evidence of the growing number of OSI-compliant products being released, OSI appears to have been a decisive and necessary initiative. There seems every prospect that the pattern of data communications in the future will be shaped by OSI: not only does OSI meet the current need for regulation in a previously unregulated area, but it also provides sufficient flexibility to incorporate the inevitable advances which will be made in the swiftly evolving field of communications technology.

This book aims to give a general introduction to OSI for engineers, students and others who need to become familiar with its concepts and terminology. The two opening chapters give an historical account of the development of data communications and describe the philosophy of layered architectures. In Chapter 3, the principles of the seven layer OSI model are explained and OSI terminology is introduced.

Each of the seven chapters which follow deals with a layer of the OSI model. The reader with a general interest in OSI is directed to the introduction and the 'requirements' section of each chapter, which give an overview of the layer in question and its functions in relation both to the model and to the data communications environment. The 'specification' section describes in detail how the layer operates to fulfil its requirements. Each chapter concludes with a discussion of the current communications technologies, if any, which comply with the OSI standards for the layer.

The final chapter reviews the present state of OSI development. It makes particular reference to the X.400 message handling system, currently the most widely available OSI-compliant implementation.

Chapter references include the relevant OSI standards and drafts for development, as published by the British Standards Institution; the equivalent ISO references are also given.

The emphasis in the current OSI standards is on connection-oriented communication between computer systems. Connectionless services are on the whole described in addenda to those standards which define the connection-oriented services, although the intention is that these addenda should be incorporated in the main body of standards as soon as possible. This book reflects the present state of OSI development and treats connection-oriented layer services as being of primary importance.

Acknowledgements

The authors, who are all employees of Admiral Computing Group plc, wish to thank Dr Ceri James, Managing Director of the company, for making available Admiral's resources, without which this book would not have been produced. We would have made slow progress without the help and support of our colleagues in Bristol — in particular, Peter Craig, Steve Lloyd and Martin Millener — who contributed in various and significant ways to the content and appearance of the finished book. Special thanks are due to Julie Knight and Nigel Murkitt for their work on the word processing and typesetting of the book.

In addition, we should like to acknowledge the assistance and information we received from Digital Equipment Corporation (DEC), ICL and Tandem Computers Limited, computer manufacturers who are currently marketing OSI-compliant products.

1 Introduction

The ability to communicate readily with each other is one which most people accept without question. We assume that if we speak or write according to a set of linguistic rules we will be able to convey information and opinions to anyone who is familiar with those same rules. The mechanics of human communication — articulating sounds as speech, forming written words on a page, using a telephone — are, once mastered, handled subconsciously by most of us. Our principal concern in the communication process is with the translation of ideas into effective and meaningful statements; we take for granted the physical processes which are essential to human communication.

In contrast, in the field of computer communications there is very little which can be assumed or taken for granted. Effective communication between two computer systems is possible only where standards exist to govern all levels of the communication process — from the manipulation of data at the highest level to the utilisation of the physical properties of transmission media at the lowest level. To date, such standards have largely been produced by individual computer manufacturers and consequently have been restricted in application. To achieve reliable communication between any two computer systems regardless of the hardware being used, a set of globally applicable standards is required. The topic of this book is such a set of standards, currently being developed under the auspices of the International Organization for Standardization (ISO) and known as *open systems interconnection* (OSI).

1.1   The Development of Data Communications

Data is the word that has come to be used as the generic description of information which is held, manipulated or communicated by electronic computers. The field of data communications is concerned with the transfer of computer information from one system to another, whether the systems are in the same room or are separated by thousands of miles.

The evolution of data communications has been closely related to that of the digital computer. As computer technology developed from the early days of batch processing systems, which were programmed using punched cards or paper tape, to today's multi-user, interactive systems, so the need for many different types of communication grew.

The most basic and necessary form of computer communication is that between the user's terminal and the computer. At its simplest, this is a hard-wired connection between the terminal and one of the computer's terminal ports, an example of a *point-to-point* link (see Figure 1.1).

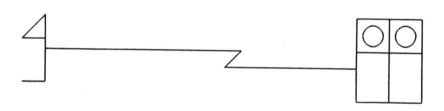

Figure 1.1 A point-to-point link

This method of providing user access to computers has obvious limitations: a user may require access to more than one computer from the same terminal; only as many terminals as there are terminal ports can be connected; a terminal occupies a port even when it is idle. To overcome these problems, *circuit-switching* can be used to provide flexible interconnection of many users with many different systems.

One familiar application of circuit-switching is the international telephone network, which is built from a number of telephone exchanges or switches linked together by point-to-point connections. This allows a subscriber to obtain a temporary connection to any other subscriber as required. In exactly the same way, a circuit-switched data communications system can be built from interconnected data exchanges or switches. Figure 1.2 shows a simple circuit switch, and Figure 1.3 shows a manually operated data switchboard, commonly called a patch panel, and similar in operation to early telephone switchboards.

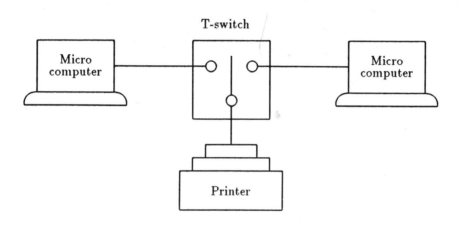

Figure 1.2 A simple circuit switch

Although the patch panel is still extensively used today for simple switching problems, an automatic method is required for cases where the users need direct control from their terminals over the switching process. The data switching equivalent of a private automatic branch exchange (PABX) is widely used for this purpose, and is termed a *data PABX*, or a *data switch*.

In conjunction with these techniques, *multiplexers* can be used to reduce the amount of cabling required, by combining data from a number of terminals onto one physical link. *Demultiplexers* are used to split the data streams at the receiving end (see Figure 1.4).

One further problem which was addressed at an early stage in the development of data communications was that of connecting geographically remote users to their computer systems. The early telegraph networks were essentially digital transmission systems, using, for example, Morse code, and could therefore be used to

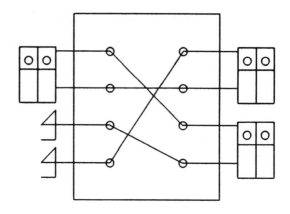

Figure 1.3 A patch panel

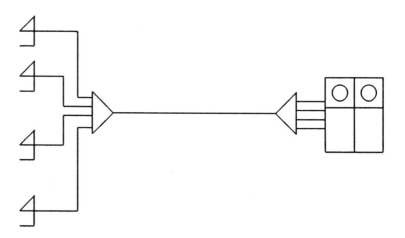

Figure 1.4 Multiplexed terminals

transmit data over long distances. These proved to be of little
help to the average computer user, since not many individuals were
connected to such networks and the networks themselves were rather
unsophisticated. However, there are many millions of subscribers to
the public switched telephone networks (PSTNs) and the networks
are geographically extensive, so they became a natural choice for
transmitting data over long distances.

Originally, PSTNs used only analogue transmission techniques,
and although digital transmission is now used extensively on trunk
routes and international circuits, the majority of subscribers still
only have an analogue line to their premises. In order to utilise
these analogue lines for the transfer of digital data, encoders and
decoders must be provided to perform the conversion of data
to voice bandwidth analogue signals and *vice versa*. *Modems*
(modulator/demodulators) convert the data into audible tones of
different frequencies at the sending end, and decode the tones into
the original data at the receiving end. This is illustrated in Figure
1.5.

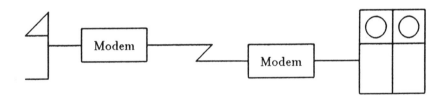

Figure 1.5 The use of modems

As products implementing these different communications techniques proliferated, it became necessary to establish standards to
govern the physical connections used between terminals, computers
and other equipment. Standards took two forms: official standards
from national standards bodies and *de facto* standards, established
by common usage. One of the earliest and now most familiar official

standards was the Electronic Industries Association Recommended Standard for transfer of data over wires, known as EIA RS-232-C, which was first defined in 1969. This standard enabled easy interfacing between different manufacturers' equipment.

Another set of standards was developed — for modems — by the International Telegraph and Telephone Consultative Committee (CCITT), a part of the United Nations Organization. The modem standards are included in a series of recommendations called the V Series, last published in 1984.

All CCITT recommendations are subject to continual scrutiny, and are updated every four years if necessary. The CCITT has responsibility for recommending standards for any equipment which may be connected to an international network, whether analogue or digital transmission is used. Where appropriate, these recommendations are normally adopted by national regulatory bodies for domestic networks. In the United Kingdom, standards are set by the British Standards Institution, and the British Approvals Board for Telecommunications (BABT) has responsibility for verifying telecommunications equipment against them.

The possibilities for high speed data communications over long-haul networks seem limitless. Currently, it is possible to transfer data from one side of the world to the other, over a series of circuit-switched point-to-point links which may be ordinary local telephone circuits, fibre optic or microwave trunk routes, or satellite links, at rates in excess of millions of bits per second. In order to open these possibilities up to computer users, a large number of products and associated regulatory standards have been developed, and this number is growing all the time.

1.2   Computer Networks

Whilst the techniques described in the previous section can be applied equally well to communications between computer systems and to communications between terminals and computers, a further set of requirements for inter-system communication evolved which was not satisfied by the provision of circuit-switched links.

These requirements are centred around a need to share information and resources amongst a number of computers, which may be close together or geographically remote from each other. Large databases (for example, bank account records) may need to be split up into a number of systems, but all the information must still be accessible to each system's users. A financial accounting package running on a mainframe may require access to a stock control system running on a minicomputer or microcomputer. A number of microcomputers may wish to share one file management system or a single disk drive.

In order to overcome these problems a number of solutions were developed. Computer networks evolved along two parallel lines: those which interconnected systems within a fairly confined area using private cabling, termed local area networks (LANs), and those which interconnected geographically remote systems, sometimes using private physical links but more commonly using a public data transmission network, termed wide area networks (WANs). Today many computer networks involve a combination of these two types (Figure 1.6).

It soon became necessary to produce more cost-effective networks by improving the efficiency of data transmission over the physical media. Traditional circuit-switching methods can make highly inefficient use of the available resources, as typical interactions between user and computer involve only intermittent transfer of small quantities of data. Likewise for computer to computer communications, the volumes of data may be larger, but data transfer still takes place on a block by block or file by file basis rather than as a continuous stream, and the data channel is idle for much of the time.

Some form of *time-division multiplexing* (TDM) was required to use the data channel more efficiently. In TDM, the available bandwidth is allocated among a number of data sources, such that each in turn uses all the bandwidth for a short period of time (called a *timeslot*). If the timeslots are rigidly allocated, the effect is the same as circuit-switching, since a particular source has a fixed data channel allocated to it for the duration of its transmissions. Modern PSTNs use such TDM techniques extensively to multiplex many telephone channels onto high speed transmission links such as optical fibres.

For efficient data communications, bandwidth needs to be allocated according to demand. In the early 1960s, a technique called

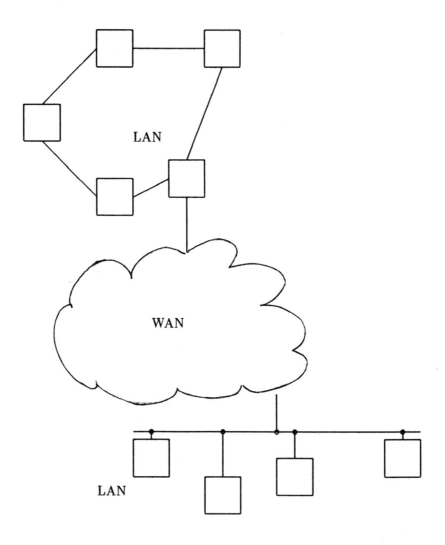

Figure 1.6 A typical computer network

packet-switching was developed in the USA for performing such an allocation. In a packet-switched network, each computer attached to the network may access a data channel on a demand basis, despatch a 'packet' of data into the network and then release the channel, freeing it for use by others.

In 1967 the Advanced Research Projects Agency (ARPA) in the USA started a network project to link all the academic and industrial research centres which were working on ARPA projects. The resulting nationwide network, called ARPANET, used packet-switching techniques and formed the basis for much subsequent work by academic communities, public communications network suppliers and manufacturers. In the LAN domain, manufacturers introduced products such as Xerox's Ethernet and IBM's Token Ring, whilst in the public domain, packet-switched data networks (PSDNs) were developed.

All these network products use packet-switching to provide efficient use of bandwidth, but they remain incompatible. Deciding which computer can access the transmission medium at any particular moment is the inherent problem of packet-switching, and each network product offers a different solution.

Inevitably, as the market for such products grew, so too did the need to establish standards for both LANs and PSDNs. The American Institute of Electrical and Electronics Engineers (IEEE) worked towards the establishment of LAN standards in its IEEE 802 Series. Although not an international organization, the IEEE has much worldwide influence through its relationship with major computer manufacturers. In the public domain, the CCITT developed a recommendation called X.25, drafted in 1976 and updated in 1980 and 1984. This provides the standards for the basic transmission and access methods for public packet-switched data networks, although many of the higher level functions apply equally well to many private networks, including LANs.

1.3 Layered Architectures

The provision of efficient transmission and switching schemes, as described in the previous section, is not in itself sufficient to allow information and resources to be shared among computer systems. In the early to mid-seventies, many computer manufacturers introduced families of network products which were designed not only to allow easy interconnection between all the computers in their own range, but also to provide the ability for the computers to *interwork*. This implies that not only can data be transferred from one system to another, but also that more than one system can cooperate in performing a particular task or set of tasks.

In order to give structure to the various levels of functions which must be provided to support interworking, most manufacturers proposed entire system architectures. IBM's System Network Architecture (SNA), DEC's Digital Network Architecture (DNA), ICL's Onion Skin Architecture and many others, were all concepts which provided a framework for network product development, and as such they were welcomed by their respective users. They were all similar in employing a concept called a *layered architecture* which is illustrated in Figure 1.7.

The concept was not a new one. ARPANET had employed a four layer model, the lowest layer being at the physical level and the highest being the user's application. The idea was to treat each layer as a 'black box', so that it could be defined and implemented separately, and so that the lower layers were 'hidden' from the user's application in the top layer. The lower layers of the various proprietary architectures were implemented using interconnection methods such as the LANs described in the previous section.

By developing all their network products according to their own architectures, manufacturers could provide some guarantee to their users that future systems would be compatible with the old ones, and that all their computer systems would interwork in a uniform way. However, there was a growing need to provide interworking between different manufacturers' equipment. This led to the development of the *gateway* concept, a gateway being an interface between different proprietary networks or between a private network and a PSDN. However, the large number of fundamentally different architectures means that the use of gateways was unattractive as a long-term solution to this problem.

At the same time, a new data communications network system was being developed by the telecommunications industry. The emergence of new technologies which allow digital transmission to be used

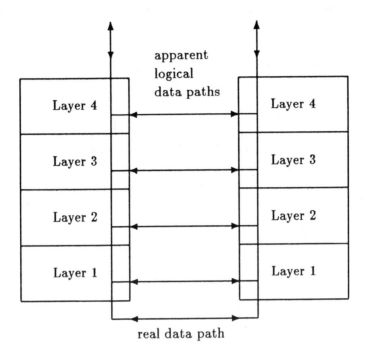

Figure 1.7 A layered architecture

throughout the PSTNs led to the definition of integrated services
digital networks (ISDNs) in the CCITT's I Series recommendations
(which are still incomplete). In an ISDN, no distinction is made
between voice and data, and it is therefore possible to join both
telephone and data subscribers by a universal network. This has
major implications, not only for existing PSDNs, but also for the
future of LAN-related products.

1.4 The ISO OSI Initiative

The existence of a number of different standards bodies, all reg-
ulating data communications from their different perspectives, has
proved to be a handicap for global standardization. In the absence
of universal standards, manufacturers have continued to develop

their own products, in order to maintain their market position. An initiative has therefore been taken by the International Organization for Standardization to unite the interests of regulatory bodies, users, and computer and telecommunications manufacturers. Its aim is to provide a forum in which universal data communications standards can be developed.

The ISO Open Systems Interconnection (OSI) basic reference model was conceived to provide a universal framework within which to develop standards for data communications products. It took six years to develop, from 1977 to 1983, and draws on existing layered architectures. The basic reference model was formulated as a seven layer architecture, with the functions of each layer selected to give maximum flexibility to implementors and to ensure that current widely-used standards could be encompassed by the model.

The introduction of the seven layer model has had a remarkable impact on the computer industry, as users now have a set of requirements which they expect their computer systems suppliers to meet. OSI conformance is likely to be an essential attribute of all future data communications products.

The following chapter gives a more detailed explanation of the layered architecture philosophy, and in particular explains how a communications system may be partitioned into layers. Subsequent chapters describe the OSI basic reference model and the details of each individual layer.

2 Philosophy of Layered Architectures

The design of a communications network which allows interconnection between many systems, manufactured by different companies, in many different locations, for a multitude of purposes, is a complex undertaking. As with any large task, the most effective way of defining and completing it successfully is to break it down into a number of smaller tasks. If the resulting tasks are still too large to be easily managed, then they too should be broken down. This process can be repeated as often as required until each portion is manageable.

One way of breaking down a large system is to split it into its constituent functions, and this is the underlying principle in *layering* as applied to the design of a communications network. Once the task has been partitioned in this way, each module can then provide its own functions to other parts of the system. For this partitioning to be useful, each module should be able to be implemented in isolation, and should have well-defined interfaces with the other modules in the system. For the problem under consideration, it is important to note that the 'system' being partitioned is in fact the network, and not a system of application programs running on the individual computers or terminals connected to the network. The functional modules into which the system may be partitioned are the different services which must be provided in order for the network to fulfil its requirements.

However, the concept of layering implies more than just an arbitrary segmentation of tasks into modules. As illustrated in Chapter 1, the partitioning may be performed in such a way that the resulting modules fit into a structure which resembles a stack of blocks (see Figure 1.7). Another view of a layered architecture is the commonly used onion skin analogy. Each skin of the onion represents a uniform layer of the architecture, and removing one layer reveals another layer which was previously completely concealed.

There is one further consideration which affects the layering process: the resulting structure must be versatile, so that it can be applied in many different situations. This is the main aim of the OSI model — to provide a framework which can be universally applied to the design of data communications networks, whether they be public or private, circuit- or packet-switched, and whether borne by wire, optical fibres, or radio waves.

In order to achieve this universal applicability, the OSI layer standards define the services provided by each layer, and how these services are to be requested by and granted to the layer above — that is, the interfaces between the layers. Each layer of the model can thus be treated as a 'black box', allowing different manufacturers of communications systems to implement the services of the layer in differing ways, whilst maintaining functional compatibility with higher layers. With the addition of standard definitions for these layer implementations, it is also possible for different manufacturers' equipment to interwork at each layer from the lowest (physical) layer upwards. Chapter 3 will examine the relationship between the OSI standards and specific implementation standards.

A number of complete sets of implementation standards have been approved within the OSI reference framework, and Chapter 11 will discuss some of these in greater detail. Here it is only important to understand that the OSI framework encompasses LANs and WANs, hybrids of the two, ISDN, packet-switching, and circuit-switching — indeed, it is intended to include any type of data communications system.

The following sections discuss the facilities required of a typical communications system, and how these may be related to a simplified layered architecture. First though, it is necessary to distinguish between the previously mentioned interfaces, and what will be called *components* here. The word 'component' has been chosen to avoid confusion with the term 'layer' used in association with the OSI model in the rest of the book.

2.1   Interfaces and Components

An interface may be described as the place (or piece of equipment or software) where interaction occurs between two systems or processes. Within the layered architecture, each layer must interact with the layer above and with the layer below. In the case of the top layer, the upwards interaction is with the user, and for the bottom layer, the downwards interaction is with the transmission medium. For each interaction an interface must be defined. Typical examples of what must be specified are:

- protocol
- timing
- any physical properties

A *protocol* in this context is a set of mutually agreed signals or messages, which are used to establish, maintain and release a communications channel between two cooperating parties. For a successful interaction, the messages exchanged must follow a defined sequence. A simple example of a protocol is the initiation of a conversation on the telephone:

- A rings B, and B picks up the telephone
- B says 'Hello, this is B' (thereby confirming to A that the call has reached the right destination)
- A says 'Hello, this is A' (thereby letting B know who is calling)

Once the above protocol has taken place, A and B can have a normal conversation. Another such protocol would be used for terminating the call (which could be much more complex than simply 'Goodbye', and 'Goodbye'). These are both examples of protocols between users of a communications system, the system in this case being a telephone network.

The *timing* used in such an interaction is also important. In the example above, A does not speak until B has confirmed that the call has reached the correct destination. However, if B fails to speak, A may decide to speak first. If B still does not speak, A will retry a small number of times, and eventually replace the handset, terminating the call. Failures which occur during such interactions in communications networks should be observable by the party which initiated the interaction, and in some cases by the recipient also, so that maintenance procedures to correct faults can be invoked.

The *physical* properties of an interface are also important. To continue our telephone analogy, one interface between the user and the telephone system is the telephone handset. The distance between the human mouth and ear constrains the size of the handset, the audio signal applied to the earpiece must be of the correct volume, and the microphone in the handset must be of the correct sensitivity for human speech. Another such interface is the telephone keypad, or the rotary dial, where again the size and shape are important, and the signals generated must be within strictly defined limits, whether they be tones or pulses. For other interfaces in communications systems, the physical properties may relate to where the interface is, either physically or logically. For most of the following discussion, interfaces are between computer programs, and the 'physical' properties of the interface may, for example, be the addresses in computer memory at which the programs access control and status information concerning their interaction.

In the diagrammatic representation of a layered architecture (see Figure 1.7), the interfaces are located at the adjacent edges of the boxes, and allow the contents of adjacent boxes to interact. The interfaces must be defined sufficiently to allow the contents of one box to request actions of, and receive the results from, its cooperating neighbours. Each box contains a logical grouping of tasks performed by the system, and this grouping is called a component here.

The remainder of this chapter will discuss the requirements of a communications system based on a simple architecture consisting of three components. This is intended to illustrate how system partitioning may take place in practice, within the layered architecture framework. This hypothetical communications architecture will consist of the following components:

- the *Network* component which is responsible for carrying the data across the network

- the *Control* component which is responsible for supervising the network as a whole

- the *User/Application* component which allows users access to network facilities

user/program

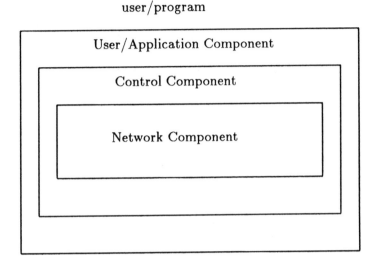

Figure 2.1 A hypothetical communications architecture

As shown in Figure 2.1, the Network Component is completely hidden by the Control Component which is in turn completely hidden from the user/program by the User/Application Component.

2.2   The Network Component

The lowest level of a communications system is the medium which carries data between two nodes of a network. Different media may be used between different pairs of nodes in the same network, but they are invisible to a user. The Network Component interfaces with the transmission medium through an appropriate transducer, which converts the data which is to be transmitted into the correct electrical, optical or radio signal, and translates received signals into the digital representation recognised by the computer or terminal.

This interface must of course be fully defined, in line with the requirements for protocol, timing and physical properties outlined in the previous section. To continue the telephone network analogy, this interface is the equivalent of that between the telephone and the twisted pair telephone cable. The shape, size and pin connections of the plugs and sockets used for this connection must be defined, as nust be the current drawn from the line by the telephone for its supply, the maximum peak-to-peak voltage of the signals sent and received and so on.

For a sophisticated data communications network, the physical interface may be complex, perhaps involving multiplexing and demultiplexing of many different data channels onto one medium, or having a series of interconnecting plugs, sockets and transducers, which repeatedly change the nature of the transmitted signal. In order for any communication to succeed, all the necessary physical connections must be made, and the transducers at either end of the medium must be fully compatible.

This compatibility must also extend to the manner in which data is manipulated during the transmission process. Data is normally stored in computer memory as bytes, or multiples of bytes. For a serial transmission method, a byte of data is sent as a number of separate bits (usually eight), starting with either the highest or the lowest order bit. It must obviously be interpreted at the receiver in the same order.

Once communication has been established between two nodes of a network at this basic level, bytes of data can be transferred from one to the other. Which bytes are transferred, and what they mean is not known by this low level network function, nor is their eventual destination beyond the next node of the network involved in this point-to-point communication.

A basic routeing function is required, and this must also be implemented by the Network Component proposed here. Returning to the telephone network analogy, routeing is performed by the network in response to the addressing information input by the user. The user needs only to know the telephone number of the required destination for the call, and uses a rotary dial or keypad to input this number. The number is translated into pulses or tones, which are transmitted over the telephone line to the local exchange, where they are decoded into a set of signals which control the switching circuits. Some further signals may be transmitted by the local exchange to a neighbouring exchange in the network, and so on until the call reaches its destination. The telephone number used here is the equivalent of a virtual address in data communications, and the network converts it into a physical address in order to perform the routeing function.

Another function which must also be performed by the network is some degree of protection against data corruption. The analogue telephone network is subject to data corruption, in the form of interference and crossed lines. Users are easily able to detect this corruption and to correct for it, if necessary by re-dialling to obtain another, less noisy line. A data communications system must have some way of detecting corruption and either correcting for it or reporting it. This may be achieved by adding redundant information to the data stream, and using it to filter out unwanted information and to guess at missing information — a similar mechanism to that used by the human brain and ear when interpreting sounds as spoken words.

One way of incorporating these functions into the communications system is to group a sequence of bytes of data together, and add extra bytes at the beginning and end of the sequence. These extra bytes may be address bytes for the source and the destination, or error checking bytes such as checksums or cyclic redundancy checks (CRCs), or simply control information to indicate the length of the sequence. Note that the routeing (addressing) information should be included in the error checking procedure, to prevent mis-routeing of data. These sequences of bytes may be called *packets*. The Network Component must be able to delimit packets contained within a continuous stream of data.

A communications system normally consists of a number of nodes connected together by point-to-point links. In the system shown in Figure 2.2, all the cities are connected to one another by at least two routes. When any node of a network transmits a packet, it needs to examine the destination address, and choose the most expedient route to that destination. Not all nodes need to know the physical address of every other node in a network; a 'general direction' may be sufficient until the packet nears its destination.

If alternative routes are available, then packets which take a short route may arrive before previously transmitted ones which have taken

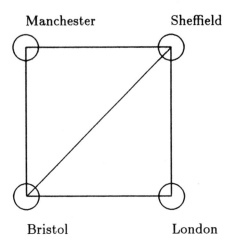

Manchester   Sheffield

Bristol   London

Figure 2.2 A communications network

a longer route. Some method is therefore required to identify the
order in which packets are despatched in order to reassemble them
in the correct order. One such method would be to add a sequence
number to each packet, possibly returning to zero after reaching a
predefined maximum.

As each packet passes through a node, checks are performed
on the error information. If a packet is missing or corrupted,
retransmission can be requested by the node, and the error reported
to the user via the Control Component.

Other techniques for routeing, such as circuit-switching, or the
establishment of 'virtual circuits' which remain open for the duration
of a communications session, may also be used. Similarly, data may
also be transmitted in duplicate via different routes to reduce the
effects of transmission errors.

In summary, the services or functions provided by the Network
Component of this hypothetical architecture are basic transport

of data through the network, routeing, and error detection and correction. The interface between the Network Component and the Control Component allows the Control Component to request establishment of data links, transfer of data and release of links. The Network Component also provides status information about data corruption and communication link failures to the Control Component, for use in its management function.

2.3   The Control Component

Whereas the Network Component is concerned primarily with the establishment and maintenance of end-to-end links, the Control Component must be concerned with management of the network as a whole. It must provide basic network services to the User/Application Component, whilst controlling the flow of data throughout the entire network. It exerts this control through its interface with the Network Component, where it requests the establishment of links, and receives status information about error conditions.

The equivalent of the Control Component in the public telephone network performs traffic management, monitoring the number of calls between each exchange, and allocating extra trunk routes via other exchanges for busy links. It is also responsible for metering each user's line, in order to levy charges for the units of call time used. These units may vary according to the distance over which the call takes place. In a private telephone network, the Control Component may also prevent unauthorised users from accessing an outside line, or from using advanced features provided by the system such as the ability to intrude onto others' calls.

In order to carry out its functions, the Control Component must be able to access information about the topology of the network. For example, any one node must know how many neighbours it has, how to address them, and the status of the links to them. The Control Component can then control congestion on busy links, if necessary by establishing alternative routes. If a prolonged communication between two nodes is required by a user, the optimum route for the data should be determined, based on knowledge about the overall network, and the Network Component should be instructed accordingly.

It is also desirable that any links which are opened by the user and then left idle, should be monitored by the system and if necessary automatically released after a specified time. The Control Component should also monitor the progress of messages through the network, to ensure that messages arrive at their destinations and to report any losses to the User/Application Component.

The network must also verify that users are authorised to access the system and that communication with the intended node is permitted. Authentication may also be required that the connection has been made with the required node, if sensitive information is to be sent. The network must have security features to ensure that no information is transmitted to unintended recipients.

The Control Component described here hides the functions of the Network Component from the User/Application Component, and provides a simple mechanism by which network connections can be requested, granted and released. It also maintains the efficiency and integrity of the network as a whole.

2.4   User/Application Component

The User/Application Component is the *raison d'être* of the entire communications system. It is the most important function in the system, since it alone is visible to users. It hides all the functionality contained in the Control and Network Components, whilst providing all the services of the network to the user.

This component must interpret the requests of the user into a form understood by the Control Component, and inform him of the status of his requests. Using the telephone network analogy, this component translates the keys depressed by the user into the pulses and tones understood by the switching circuits, and generates audible tones to indicate call progress, for example the ringing, engaged, and number unobtainable signals.

In a data communications system, the services provided can involve a more complex User/Application Component. For example, it may be necessary to transfer a file from one computer to another one in the network. In order to carry this out, the User/Application Component must first request the Control Component to open a communications link with the destination computer. Once this has been provided, it must invoke the User/Application Component in the destination computer which receives files. Data may then be transferred from the local file to the remote computer, through the Control and Network Components.

It may be the case that the local computer is of a different type from the remote one, and it may have a different way of structuring files, or of storing them. For example, it may use a different type of disk drive, or it may use a different internal representation for user data such as text. These differences should remain invisible to the user. The User/Application Component should take responsibility for interfacing with local file stores, and for formatting foreign data into the local representation. One example of this difference in data format is that between the EBCDIC and the ASCII character sets for text. The former uses an eight bit character representation, whilst the latter uses only seven.

Another consideration for any universal communications system, is that it must be able to connect users to programs, users to users, and programs to programs. Normally, users interact with a system by means of a terminal of some sort. The User/Application Component is responsible for providing the functionality associated with this man-machine interface. Normally, the interface is implemented by giving prompts on a VDU, and interpreting responses typed in on a keyboard. All types of terminals should be allowed for, and the user must be provided with the necessary prompts to allow access to all programs or services, preferably in a fashion which is uniform across all terminals and for all programs. The man-machine interface itself is not normally included in the overall communications system architecture.

In summary, the User/Application Component provides the interface between the user and the network, and allows access to the facilities provided by the network in a uniform manner, consistent across all machines in the network.

2.5   The Philosophy

This chapter has presented a hypothetical architecture for a communications system. In order to illustrate the principles of layering,

an overview of the requirements for a communications network has
been given, broken down by function into three main components.
However, each component described here itself encompasses a number of functions, which may be implemented in different ways. In
order to provide a model architecture which is universally applicable,
every function that can independently vary in implementation must
be represented by its own 'black box'.

   The OSI model is such an architecture; the three components of
the model used in this chapter are subdivided by function to give
the seven layer OSI basic reference model. The individual layers
are listed in Figure 2.3, and the model's conventional diagrammatic
representation is shown in Figure 2.4.

Layer 1	Physical Layer	Interconnection with the physical medium
Layer 2	Data Link Layer	Point-to-point transfer of data with error handling
Layer 3	Network Layer	Network control and routeing of data
Layer 4	Transport Layer	Transparent transfer of data across the network from end system to end system
Layer 5	Session Layer	Setting up and closing down of communications sessions and synchronization of data transfer
Layer 6	Presentation Layer	Data format conversion
Layer 7	Application Layer	Interface with end-user applications

Figure 2.3 The seven layers of the OSI model

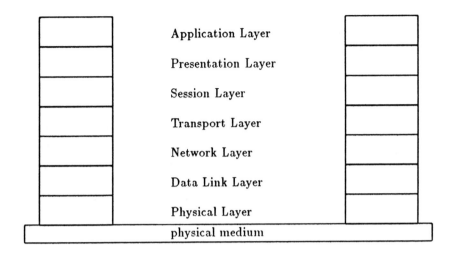

Figure 2.4 Diagrammatic representation of the OSI model

The next chapter introduces the OSI model, giving a brief outline of its history and continuing evolution, and describing the fundamental concepts which are common to each OSI layer and its interfaces. This is essential background information to each of Chapters 4 to 10 which deal with the individual layers, since it introduces the terminology and representations which apply to all layers of the OSI model.

3 The OSI Model

The preceding chapter has discussed the philosophy of layered communications architectures, and the functions which should be performed within such an architecture. It is appropriate now to focus on the seven layer OSI basic reference model as defined by the International Organization for Standardization (ISO).

Within the OSI model, each layer is responsible for providing a set of services to enable the process of communication to take place. While the functions of the individual layers are markedly different, individual tasks in different layers are often performed in a similar manner. In order to stress the importance of OSI as an ordered architecture (and to avoid unnecessary repetition), these common areas are described in general terms in this chapter. The chapters which follow contain detailed descriptions of the operation of the individual layers, but they assume a familiarity with the overall concepts of OSI and its terminology which are set out here.

3.1 OSI Standards

The ISO is responsible for the production of internationally recognised standards: to this end it coordinates the activities of national standards bodies, such as the British Standards Institution (BSI), and of technically oriented standing committees, such as the CCITT, the European Computer Manufacturers Association (ECMA) and the Conference of European Postal and Telecommunications Administrations (CEPT). These bodies in turn provide a forum for the ideas and opinions of parties with an interest in the particular area of standardization under development. In the case of the OSI model, for example, input has come principally from the CCITT, representing the interests of national telecommunications utilities, especially for the lower layers.

When a standard has been ratified by the ISO, it is in effect returned to the national standards organizations for implementation.

Thus the BSI has published a document, *Basic reference model for open systems interconnection* (Reference 3.1), which is identical with the previously ratified ISO standard describing the OSI model. Associated with this document are numerous standards, draft standards and recommendations which provide the basis for commercial implementations of OSI. These documents detail the functions of the individual layers which make up the OSI model and in some cases (the CCITT X.400 message handling system (MHS) group of recommendations is an example) establish the implementation specification for actual operations within the framework established by the OSI model.

The relationship between the reference model defined in Reference 3.1, the layer standards and the implementation specifications is a potentially confusing one. The reference model sets out the architecture and philosophy to which the layer standards must adhere. The layer standards in turn describe the functions of the individual layers and provide the detailed requirements against which implementation specifications can be drawn up.

Where a layer standard postdates an implementation specification for that layer, some degree of accommodation between the standard and the implementation specification needs to take place. In the case of the Network Layer and X.25 packet-switching, for example, it was necessary to draw up the layer standard sufficiently broadly to include X.25; at the same time, X.25 was modified to make it comply more closely with the requirements of the OSI Network Layer. Where a layer standard describes functions which are not covered by any existing implementation specification, the layer can be defined in a more idealised form. It is then the responsibility of implementors to match the OSI standards, and not *vice versa*.

Compliance of commercially available products can be tested against a particular implementation specification, such as X.400. The implementation specification can be checked for conformance with the relevant OSI layer standards, which should adhere in all respects to the architecture and philosophy of the OSI reference model. A product may conform with OSI in that it embodies the concepts of a layered architecture expressed in Reference 3.1. It may contain seven layers which perform functions identical with those of the OSI layers. If, however, its protocols do not comply with the OSI specification, it cannot be classed as an OSI-compliant product.

3.2   Implementing OSI

When considering how OSI may be implemented, it is essential to take an objective look at what the OSI model offers to potential implementors. In general terms, it is simply a model of a layered communications architecture and thereby serves to state a philosophy for the regulation of communication between computer systems. While the standards describe the functions and operations of the layers in greater detail, they do not specify the exact method of implementation. The products of computer manufacturers which claim compliance with OSI standards are, therefore, markedly different in their internal operation. OSI insists only that the functions performed by these products, their interfaces and their protocols, should be consistent with the standards.

There is a further cautionary point which must be raised, relating to the state of completeness of OSI. OSI covers a hugely diverse and complex area of technology; the interests, some of them conflicting, of many parties have to be considered in drawing up the international standards. It follows that OSI has developed over a number of years, its progress marked by a series of standards and discussion documents. In some cases, the detailed standards preceded the definition of the OSI model as a whole. Of the seven layers of the OSI model, some are more fully specified than others. In particular, Layers 1 to 4, which deal largely with the physical transfer of data across circuits and networks, are further advanced than Layers 5 to 7, which enable data to be presented to applications in an orderly manner. Specifying the attributes of a length of wire and a couple of plugs is less taxing than specifying the requirements for a file transfer protocol, and the standards makers have concentrated on those parts of OSI which can most easily be agreed and documented. Manufacturers have followed the course set by the standards: while there are many products which claim to comply with the requirements of the Physical Layer (Layer 1), there are none, as yet, which could claim to implement all the possible facilities of the Application Layer (Layer 7).

These apparent deficiencies in OSI demonstrate one of its

principal strengths as a potential industry standard for the next few decades. Once the concept of a layered architecture has been agreed along with a broad outline of the functions to be performed by each layer, it is then possible to develop the layers in isolation. A change to the requirements for a particular layer some time in the future will not alter the validity of the model as a whole; nor will it have an impact on other layers within the model, except perhaps on the immediate neighbours of the modified layer.

It is this feature of OSI which has given manufacturers the confidence to develop products for the lower layers, knowing that their products will not suddenly be made redundant by changes in the layers above. These partial implementations of OSI support products which may correspond in function to the upper layers of OSI, but do not necessarily comply with the OSI standards. It is to be expected that partial implementations will evolve into full implementations of OSI as manufacturers follow up the continuing ratification of new standards with further OSI-compliant products. In the meanwhile, however, two partial implementations will be able to communicate using OSI standard protocols, to the extent shown in Figure 3.1.

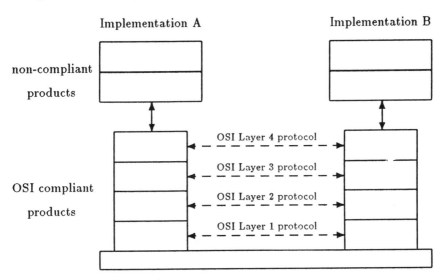

Figure 3.1 Partial implementations of OSI

3.3   What is Open Systems Interconnection?

Twentieth century man relies upon systems — collections of tasks integrated to produce the required output from a given set of inputs. These tasks may be performed manually, electronically or mechanically. Getting money from a bank's cash dispenser involves manual input of a card and entry of a personal identification number (PIN), manual selection of a sum of money, electronic processing of the transaction details, and mechanical dispensing of the cash. In OSI terminology, this is a *real* system — that is, it consists of all the processes and operations which result in the correct sum of money being dispensed to the bank's customer.

The cash dispenser system may be self-contained and separate from any other system which the bank happens to possess. It is more probable, however, that the dispenser is linked in some way to other bank systems, those managing credit and debit entries on customer accounts, for example, or providing up to date statements of account balances. If the cash dispenser system can be connected to other systems in compliance with the OSI standards, it can claim to be a real *open* system as distinct from all interconnected real systems which do not comply with OSI.

The OSI standards define only those parts of real open systems which are relevant to communication between systems. In the example of the cash dispenser, manual and mechanical tasks are outside the scope of OSI. When these and other irrelevant tasks have been stripped away, the remaining *open system* is all that we, and OSI, are concerned with (see Figure 3.2).

So far, 'OSI' has been used loosely to cover the field of communication between computer systems. The initials 'OSI' stand for 'open systems interconnection', and it is important to emphasise the significance of *interconnection* in this context. Communication implies a fairly passive transfer of information between systems; interconnection has been chosen because OSI allows a more active relationship between systems. This is sometimes referred to as the ability to *interwork* — as an example, an application in one open system may be started, controlled and terminated by an application in another open system. Within OSI, the cash dispenser system would have the potential to initiate and manage applications in other

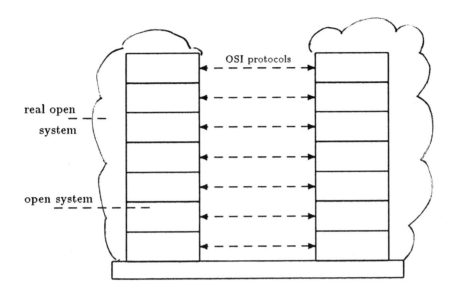

Figure 3.2 Open systems

OSI systems to which it was connected — the customer account maintenance system, for example. (How the other system performed its account maintenance tasks would be of no concern to OSI.)

It has been stated previously that the lower layers of the OSI model are the furthest advanced in terms of their detailed specification and implementation. In spite of this, it must be remembered that OSI exists primarily to provide a service for applications which are located in the uppermost layer. Viewed from the outside, then, a pair of interconnected open systems would appear as shown in Figure 3.3 — an application in one open system connected by means of some physical medium to an application in a second open system. The activity which must take place in the layers below the applications in order to make the connection is of as little concern to the applications as is the internal operation of a telephone exchange to the average telephone user.

3.4 Operation within the OSI Layered Architecture

A full OSI open system consists of seven *subsystems*, arranged hierarchically, with applications at the top of the pile and the

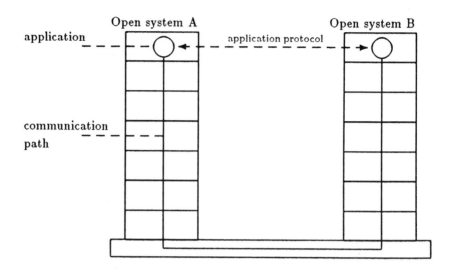

Figure 3.3 High level view of open systems interconnection

physical communications link at the bottom. Any subsystem can communicate only with its two immediate neighbours and then only by means of a common interface (see Figure 3.4). The top and bottom subsystems are restricted to communication with one other subsystem only.

Subsystems at any given level constitute a *layer*. Thus the application subsystems of Open System A and of Open System B are components of the Application Layer. Figure 3.5 demonstrates this relationship between subsystem and layer and also introduces the concept of the (N)-Layer and (N)-notation. The (N)-Layer can be any layer within the OSI model; it provides (N)-services, for example, and utilises an (N)-protocol. The (N)-notation provides a convenient way of describing in general terms those features of the OSI model which are common across layers, particularly the way in which neighbouring layers interact.

Each subsystem consists of one or more functional elements, called *entities*. What actually constitutes an entity depends on the function it performs and the layer in which it is located. It

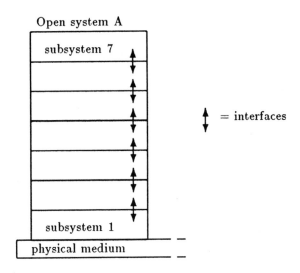

Figure 3.4 Communication between subsystems

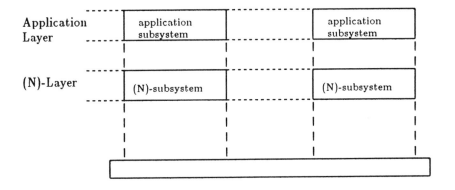

Figure 3.5 (N)-subsystems and (N)-layers

might, for example, be a software package running on a piece of communications hardware and complying in its operation with the relevant OSI standards. An entity should be distinguished from a *process* (which can be defined as a course of action leading to some predetermined end). In the terminology of OSI, processes have functions beyond the area defined by OSI; entities are the OSI-related parts of processes. In the Application Layer, processes and entities have a slightly different relationship from that which exists in the lower layers, a difference which is explained in Chapter 10.

The Application Layer is composed of application entities; the (N)-Layer, using the (N)-notation, is composed of (N)-entities. The entities within a given layer (peer-entities) combine to provide a service for the layer above. In the (N)-Layer, therefore, the (N)-entities cooperate in providing the (N)-service to the (N+1)-Layer.

The primary service which (N)-entities are designed to provide is the establishment of a *connection* between the (N+1)-entities sitting above them in the stack. (This chapter does not take account of the possibility of *connectionless* communication, which is currently being incorporated in OSI.) Connection between peer-entities assumes a horizontal link, but it must still be achieved by means of communication vertically through the common interfaces, which is the only direction of data transfer allowed within OSI. For two (N+1)-entities to be connected, an (N)-connection must be established between them through the (N)-Layer (see Figure 3.6).

The (N)-connection is governed by a set of rules known as the (N)-protocol. The (N)-protocol provides the apparent horizontal link between peer-entities, as distinct from the actual vertical communication path established through the interfaces which exist between layers. Taking the Presentation and Session layers as an example, it can be seen that:

- *presentation entities* can be connected only by means of a *session connection*

- *session entities* cooperate to provide the *session service* to presentation entities in the Presentation Layer

- a *session protocol* exists to govern the interaction between the cooperating session entities

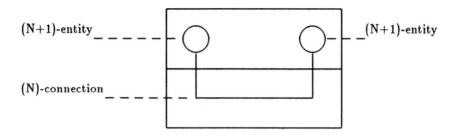

Figure 3.6 The (N)-connection

For the session entities to have cooperated in establishing the session connection, they too must have been connected — in their case, through a transport connection provided by the Transport Layer. Indeed, to achieve the apparently simple task of enabling two applications to communicate, a series of connections must have been made for all layers from the lowest layer upwards (see Figure 3.7). It should be noted that, as there is no layer above the Application Layer, there can be no application connection. When application entities are connected by means of a presentation connection, they are said to be *associated*.

When the applications have completed their tasks and no longer need to communicate, the process of connection is reversed and the connections are released. There is no need, however, for all connections to be released: it may be desirable to retain connections in the lower layers, in anticipation of further requests for connection from the application processes above them. Note that activity in lower layers is concealed from layers above. As far as an application entity is concerned, it simply asks a presentation entity for a connection to be established or released and is unaware of the effort required to meet its request. Similarly, as shown in Figure 3.7, the associated application entities believe they are communicating directly with each other by means of the OSI application protocols, whereas the real line of communication runs through all the layers below them.

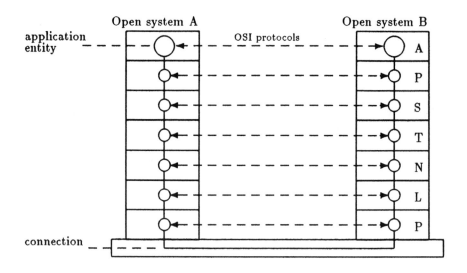

Figure 3.7 Establishing a connection between application entities

In some environments, it may be necessary for two open systems to make use of intermediate open systems to establish a connection (see Figure 3.8). The intermediate open systems consist only of the three lowest layers (Network Layer, Data Link Layer and Physical Layer) and act as relays, handling the lower level data transfer between the two end open systems.

It has been shown that for two systems to be connected, a series of connections must be established linking entities within all layers of the two connected systems. The process of linkage is started from within the Application Layer. Assume that an application entity wishes to communicate with an application entity in another open system. To achieve this, it must ask the Presentation Layer for one of its presentation services, in this case the connection establishment service. The application entity will then be linked to the presentation entity which can provide that service, and it in turn will request a link to the appropriate session entity. This process is repeated down through the layers of the initiating system until the physical medium is reached, and then up through the layers of the receiving system until the two application entities are connected. They can now

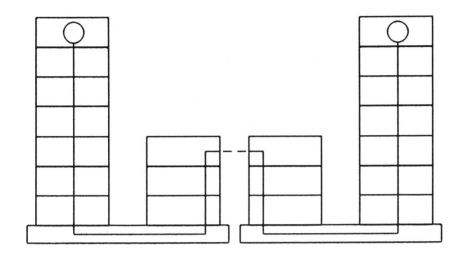

Figure 3.8 Intermediate open systems

communicate with each other, and in so doing will call upon other presentation services. Finally, the connection will be terminated, again by means of a presentation service.

For an (N)-entity to request a service from the layer below, the appropriate (N-1)-entity must be identified by a process of selection and routeing between the two layers. This is achieved by means of an *(N-1)-service access point,* in effect the point on the interface between the (N)- and (N-1)-Layers at which the entities are attached. A service access point is known by its service access point address, abbreviated to *address.* Within the (N-1)-service access point are one or more *(N-1)-connection endpoints;* an (N-1)-connection endpoint is the terminator of an (N-1)-connection and is known by its connection endpoint identifier. Entities may have multiple links with other entities in the layers above and below, but an (N-1)-service access point can be linked only to one (N)-entity and one (N-1)-entity at a given time. The relationship between entities and service access points is shown in Figure 3.9.

The management of addresses is a complex part of the function of a layer, and as such a detailed account is outside the scope

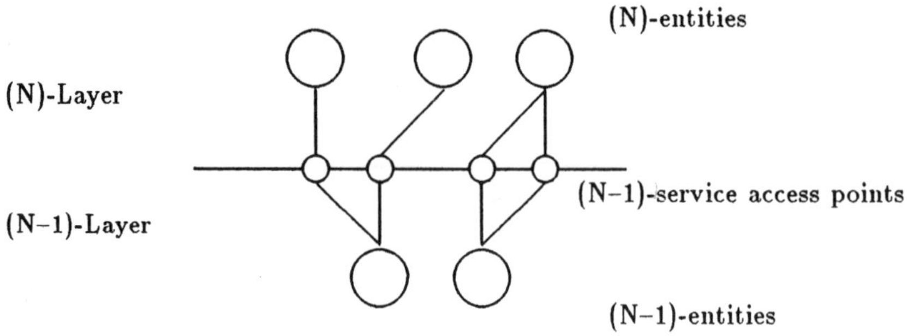

Figure 3.9 Entities connected via service access points

of this chapter. All that need be said here is that some entities are permanently associated with a single address and that others may be associated with a variety of addresses: in the first case routeing between addresses is relatively straightforward; in the second, routeing must be accomplished using address tables or by some other means.

Peer-entities and entities in adjacent layers exchange a variety of kinds of information. Three broad classes of transferred information can be identified:

- interface control information (ICI)
- protocol control information (PCI)
- user data (UD)

Interface control information is transferred between the (N)-entity and the (N–1)-entity to ensure that their cooperation across the layer interface proceeds smoothly. *Protocol control information* is transferred between (N)-entities through the (N–1)-connection to establish and maintain their joint operation. *User data* is the information which is transferred between peer-entities; its transfer is the justification for establishing the connection between entities.

The messages which are passed between entities, termed *data units*, are made up of a combination of classes of information, the exact make-up depending on the function of the data unit in the communication process. User data is combined with protocol control information to provide a *protocol data unit* (PDU), the data unit which is transferred between peer-entities. The protocol data unit is combined with interface control information, to provide the *interface data unit* (IDU), the data unit which is transferred across the interface between entities in adjacent layers. Figure 3.10 details this process of combination.

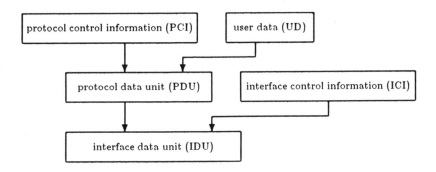

Figure 3.10 PDUs and IDUs

When the IDU has been transferred across the interface, the interface control information is no longer required and can be stripped away to leave the *service data unit* (SDU). Protocol control information combined with user data in one layer thus becomes the service data unit in the layer below. It should be noted that the (N)-SDU is the core of data which is passed intact from one end of the (N)-connection to the other. Figure 3.11 shows the relationship between PDUs, IDUs and SDUs.

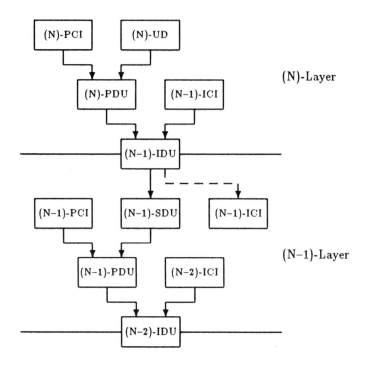

Figure 3.11 Data units and their relationship

The service data unit grows in size as it is transferred downwards from layer to layer, each layer adding its own protocol control information to the SDU it receives. This process of successive addition is known as *enveloping*, a term which usefully conveys the idea of a vital core of user data being enclosed in successive envelopes of protocol control information. When complete, the package is transferred across the physical medium to the receiving open system. Here, each layer in turn opens one of the envelopes to extract the appropriate protocol control information before passing the remains of the package on to the layer above.

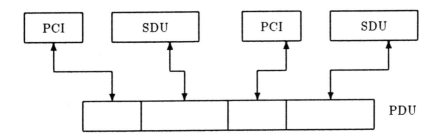

Figure 3.12 Blocking and deblocking

In some situations it is convenient for an entity to *block* more than one service data unit into a single protocol data unit. As can be seen in Figure 3.12, the individual SDUs are associated with their own protocol control information within the blocked PDU. The PDU must later be *deblocked* to extract the component SDUs.

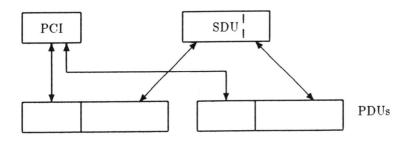

Figure 3.13 Segmenting and reassembling

The opposite situation may also occur, as shown in Figure 3.13, where it is convenient to *segment* a single service data unit into several protocol data units. In this case, each PDU contains a part of the SDU together with protocol control information. The PDUs must later be *reassembled* to restore the original SDU.

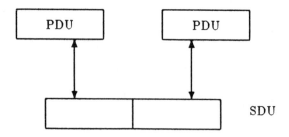

Figure 3.14 Concatenation and separation

Yet another possibility is the process of *concatenation* and *separation*, where multiple (N)-PDUs are concatenated into one (N–1)-SDU as shown in Figure 3.14. The SDU is later separated into its component PDUs.

Connections between entities may be managed in a similar way, as shown in Figure 3.15. A single (N)-connection may be *split* by an (N)-entity to yield several (N–1)-connections; later these (N–1)-connections will be *recombined* to restore the single (N)-connection. Alternatively, a connection may be provided more efficiently if several (N)-connections are *multiplexed* by an (N)-entity to produce a single (N–1)-connection; this connection will be *demultiplexed* to restore the multiple (N)-connections.

When peer-entities are communicating, they make use of a variety of services in the layer beneath them. These services are provided by the exchange of protocol data units within the layer and by a number of elementary functions, called *primitives*, which involve an exchange of messages between entities in adjacent layers. Primitives are of four types:

- request primitive — used by an initiating (N+1)-entity to request an (N)-service

- indication primitive — used by an (N)-entity to indicate to a receiving (N+1)-entity that a request for an (N)-service has been issued by a remote (N+1)-entity

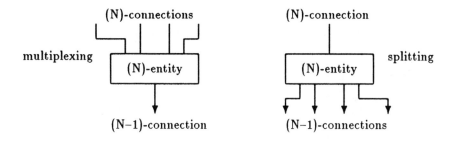

Figure 3.15 Multiplexing and splitting

- response primitive — used by a receiving (N+1)-entity to respond to an indication primitive

- confirm primitive — used by an (N)-entity to confirm to the initiating (N+1)-entity that a previously requested service has been provided

Primitives are used in various combinations to provide the individual layer services, of which there are three types. The first is the *confirmed* service, where the initiating entity is informed that the service it has requested has been successfully performed. The second is the *unconfirmed* service, where no confirmation is given that the service has been performed. The third type of service is the *provider-initiated* service, where the layer providing a connection takes it upon itself to initiate a primitive for the benefit of the connected entities in the layer above.

Figure 3.16 shows a typical exchange of primitives and protocol data units to provide a confirmed service. This diagrammatic representation will be used throughout the book to illustrate services provided by the individual layers. Time sequence diagrams are commonly used in the OSI standards to show the relationship of primitive events against time. Figure 3.17 (a) represents the sequence of primitives typically required for a confirmed service, while Figure 3.17 (b) illustrates an unconfirmed service.

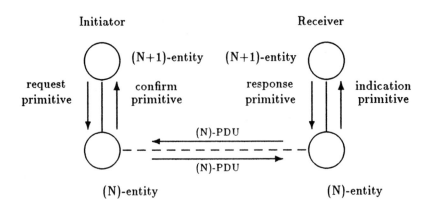

Figure 3.16 Exchange of primitives to provide a confirmed service

3.5   Formal Methods for Describing OSI Layer Operation

A layer is a collection of entities in a complex relationship with each other and with entities in adjacent layers. Entities *act* in response to *events* — the information and instructions (in the form of data units) which they receive. Their action is further determined by the *state* they are in when the request for action is received. The operation of a layer, where entities may be in one of many states and in receipt of one of many instructions, allows for a multitude of possible actions. A successful way of representing this complexity of operation is by means of a *protocol machine* supported by a *finite state machine*. The protocol machine can be imagined as a model of the working parts of the layer; the finite state machine is a table of states, events and consequent actions which describes how the protocol machine will behave in a given set of circumstances. A fictional example of a finite state machine is given in Figure 3.18.

While Figure 3.18 represents only a fragment of what such a table would look like in practice, it nevertheless serves to show how the actions to be performed (which include transition from one state to another) are dependent upon a combination of state and events. Layer operation may also be described using *formal*

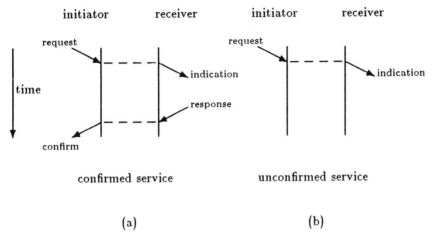

Figure 3.17 Time sequences of primitives

description techniques (FDTs) which allow the behaviour of a system to be defined without reliance upon a natural language, such as English. The system is described instead by defining the relationship between events in formal mathematical terms. The application of this technique to a reference model, such as OSI, has obvious benefits: LOTOS (Language of Temporal Ordering Specification) is an FDT which has been developed specifically for OSI. Together with the use of finite state machines, LOTOS allows layer operation to be described unambiguously and provides the basis for testing products for compliance with the layer standards.

This chapter has concentrated on showing how the OSI seven layer model provides a general framework for the transfer of data through and between open systems. The following chapters describe the individual layers in detail, each chapter stating the requirements for the layer and then discussing how the layer operates in meeting those requirements. The significant services provided by the layer (for example, connection establishment, data transfer and connection release) are explained, together with the protocols associated with those services. In this context, error handling within OSI is mentioned but the emphasis is on explaining the details of normal

STATE EVENT	CLOSED (state 1)	OPEN (state 2)
REQUEST OPEN	perform OPEN go to state 2	return error stay in state 2
REQUEST CLOSE	return error stay in state 1	perform CLOSE go to state 1

Figure 3.18 Finite state machine

operation. Each chapter concludes with an account of the current state of development of the layer, in terms both of the standards and of the products which implement those standards — a reminder that OSI is quickly moving towards acceptance as the industry standard for computer communications.

3.6   Reference

3.1 *Basic reference model for open systems interconnection*
(BS 6568), British Standards Institution, 1984. (This standard is the equivalent of ISO 7498.)

4 Physical Layer – Layer 1

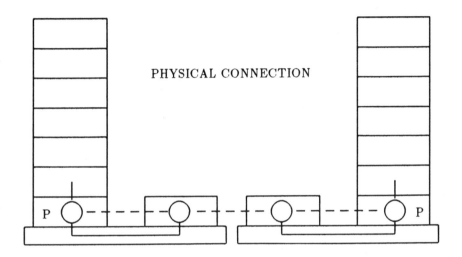

PHYSICAL CONNECTION

The Physical Layer is the lowest layer in the OSI model, and is the only layer where a subsystem in one open system communicates directly with the corresponding subsystem in another. Its function is to transfer information transparently between physical service users (data link entities). This transfer is implemented by the transmission of bit streams over a physical medium.

The Physical Layer's functions may be summarised as follows:

- activation, maintenance and deactivation of physical connections (including relay of connections)
- transmission of physical service data units (physical SDUs) either synchronously or asynchronously
- management of the Physical Layer services

These functions are provided by appropriate protocols between

47

Physical Layer entities, which are interconnected through the use
of electrical and mechanical connections to the physical medium.

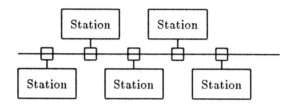

Figure 4.1 A bus topology

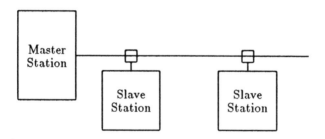

Figure 4.2 Multipoint topology with master and slave stations

A physical connection between data link entities may be made
either over a single end-to-end connection or, where several data
link entities share the same physical medium, by using multipoint
connections. Figures 4.1 to 4.3 show topologies for the connection
of workstations to the physical medium which are commonly used in
LANs.

The CSMA/CD (carrier sense multiple access and collision detection) and Token Bus technologies use the bus topology illustrated in
Figure 4.1. In the multipoint topology shown in Figure 4.2, several
stations share the same medium, with one master station having
the capability to communicate with one or more slave stations. The

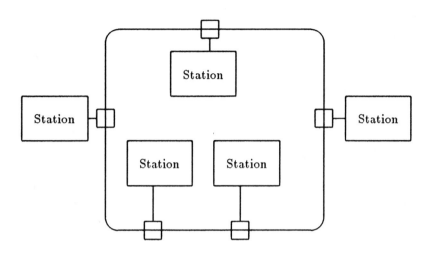

Figure 4.3 A ring topology

ring topology shown in Figure 4.3 is used in the Token Ring LAN standard. These different technologies are discussed in more detail in section 4.3.

As the Physical Layer provides a transparent service for data transfer, it has no knowledge or control over the data being transmitted. Thus higher layers may use a single physical medium to support a number of logical connections. In this way, the Network Layer multiplexes a number of logical channels over a single physical medium.

At the boundary between the Physical Layer and the physical medium, a logical connection termed the *physical media connection* is defined by OSI. However, the actual mechanical, electromagnetic and other media-dependent characteristics of this real connection are specified only by the relevant technology standards, as are the media types which are used to transport the data. These media types may be:

- twisted pair cables
- coaxial cable
- fibre optic

- microwave

- radio

4.1   Requirements for Layer 1

The Physical Layer must provide for the transparent transmission of bit streams between data link entities across physical connections. A physical SDU comprises one bit when the transmission is serial, or n bits when the transmission is in parallel. For the remainder of this chapter, serial transmission will be assumed with the corresponding single bit physical SDU. Single bit physical SDUs may be combined with others to form bit streams which may be transmitted by either duplex or half duplex techniques. The Physical Layer always delivers bits in the same order as they were transmitted.

Physical connection endpoint identifiers must be provided by the Physical Layer to allow the data link entity to identify physical connection endpoints. A physical connection may have two or more endpoints. A simple point-to-point connection has two endpoints only, whereas a multipoint connection has as many endpoints as there are connected systems.

The communications path between physical entities through the physical medium is termed a *data circuit*. The Physical Layer must provide *data circuit identification*, which is passed through the Data Link Layer to the Network Layer where it is used to identify data circuits in adjacent open systems. A number of data circuits may be connected in series by means of the relaying functions in the Physical Layer; the process of data circuit connection is controlled from the Data Link Layer.

Fault and error conditions must be notified to the data link entity which, if not corrected by the Data Link Layer, may in turn be notified to the network entity in the case of corrective action (such as re-routeing) being required.

The *quality of service* (QOS) provided by a physical connection is dependent on its constituent data circuits, the main parameters being:

- error rate
- availability

- transmission rate

- transit delay

Facilities are also required to provide synchronization of the data over the physical medium, both when transmitting and receiving the individual bits. Additional facilities are required when half duplex transmission is used, to control which end of the link is allowed to transmit at any given time.

The data may be transmitted over the physical medium either synchronously or asynchronously: asynchronous transmission uses start and stop bits to delineate groups of bits whereas synchronous transmission transmits only the data bits (using a clock to identify the individual bits).

RTS — REQUEST TO SEND
RFS — READY FOR SENDING
CI — CALLING INDICATOR
DTR — DATA TERMINAL READY

Figure 4.4 Examples of V.24 parallel circuits

Either parallel or serial circuits may be used to transmit physical protocol data units (physical PDUs). In the case of parallel media, separate wires are used, as shown in Figure 4.4, to perform control and data transmission functions. For serial media, control information must be embedded in the serial stream of data bits. It should be noted that even where parallel media are used, as in V.24, data transmission is normally still serial.

4.2 Specification of Layer 1

The OSI model was developed after the majority of physical data transmission techniques, and therefore implementations of the Physical Layer are more diverse and more widely established than implementations of the higher layers. As the existing implementations of the Physical Layer are described in their own terminology, this section will use the terminology of OSI to define the functions of the layer.

The basic function of the Physical Layer is to provide a transparent transmission service for streams of bits. In addition it must provide facilities to control the flow of the bits, and also the synchronization required to identify individual bits in the data flow.

Due to the diversity of implementations of the Physical Layer and of the functions which it provides, OSI does not categorise Physical Layer services into connectionless and connection-oriented operation. The provision of a physical connection between two or more data link entities is required by the basic reference model, however, and this is a connection-oriented concept. Implementations which do not provide such connections explicitly, but which provide a data transfer service between two data link entities, are operating in an OSI connectionless mode.

Connection-oriented data transfer requires that a physical connection first be activated between two or more data link entities. In order for this to take place, primitives must be exchanged between the relevant data link and physical entities, accompanied by interactions between physical entities over data circuits. These interactions are the exchange of physical PDUs — that is, the use of Physical Layer protocols. These protocols are defined by the relevant technology standards. Typically, the exchanges illustrated in Figure 4.5 would take place to provide the Physical Connection Activation service, over a point-to-point link.

The activation of a physical connection may require the activation of one or more data circuits. Alternatively, data circuits may be set up when the communications equipment is powered on, and released only when the equipment is powered off. An activated data circuit exists when bits may be exchanged between the two physical entities. For this to be possible, the Physical Layer must provide facilities for converting bits into signals suitable for transmission over the medium, and the corresponding inverse facilities for converting

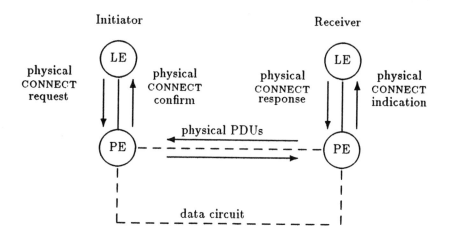

Figure 4.5 Activating a physical connection

received signals back into bits. The methods used to provide these facilities are not covered here, but further explanations may be found in many standard text books on data communications.

Once a physical connection has been activated, physical SDUs may be transmitted using the Data Transfer service. As physical SDUs are normally single bits, it is unlikely that any implementation would require acknowledgement of receipt of data from the remote physical entity. The physical entity may use the DATA confirm primitive to indicate that data transfer is complete, and that it is ready to accept more data.

Connectionless data transfer may take place without the activation of a physical connection. In this case, the data link entity uses a DATA request primitive to transmit data directly over a data circuit without the need for connection activation protocols to be exchanged, and receives a DATA indication primitive from the physical entity when data arrives for it. The DATA confirm primitive would be used as for the connection-oriented service. Connectionless data transfer is illustrated in Figure 4.6.

Connectionless data transfer is used in networks such as LANs,

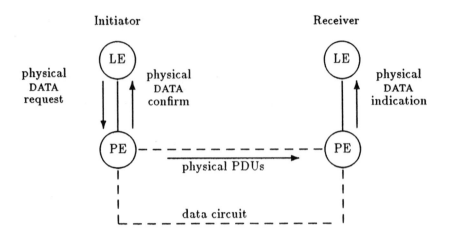

Figure 4.6 Connectionless data transfer

where data being transmitted by one physical entity is broadcast across the physical medium, received by all physical entities which are connected to the medium, and passed to the Data Link Layer unchanged. The Data Link Layer and the layers above are then responsible for accepting and responding to data destined for them. A service is provided to the Data Link Layer which indicates to it the status of the physical medium, rather than the status of a particular physical entity attached to the medium.

The Reset service may be used by the data link entity if it detects unusually high error rates or requires to resynchronize the physical connection. The physical entity may also initiate the Reset service if the quality of the physical medium deteriorates, or to inform the data link entity that a temporary loss of connection (and consequent loss of data) has occurred.

Physical connections may be deactivated through the use of DIS-CONNECT primitives. Deactivation may be initiated by a data link entity when it no longer requires the physical connection. In the case

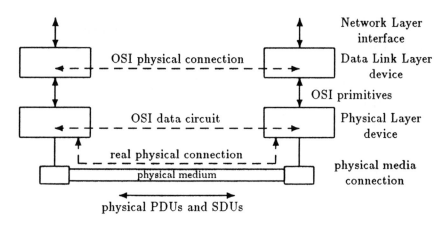

Figure 4.7 Real physical connections

of catastrophic failure of the physical medium, the physical entities may inititiate deactivation, by passing DISCONNECT indications to their data link entities.

In real open systems, the boundary between the Data Link Layer and the Physical Layer is often the interface between two integrated circuits, and the primitives exchanged across the boundary are control signals passing between the two devices. Similarly the protocols used between two cooperating physical entities to activate, maintain and deactivate data circuits are often implemented through signals passing between the local and remote Physical Layer devices. These signals are transported by the physical medium, which is connected to the physical entities by real physical connections. Frequently, these latter connections are made on a semi-permanent basis when communications equipment is installed or powered up. Figure 4.7 shows the relationship between the bottom two layers and a real implementation similar to that described above.

4.3   Discussion of Technologies

In the lower layers, existing technologies do not always map directly onto the OSI model. This section does not pretend to be an authoritative reference work on the technologies covered, but discusses those

parts of common technologies which correspond with the Physical
Layer. The technologies discussed here are:

- V.24/V.28 (including V Series modems)
- X.21 bis
- X.21
- ISDN
- CSMA/CD
- Token Ring and Token Bus

The CCITT recommendations *V.24* and *V.28*, and the similar
standard EIA RS-232-C, are probably the most commonly used
standards for interfacing data communications equipment. The connection to the physical medium is normally by means of the familiar
D-Type 25 pin plug and socket. The CCITT recommendations are
particularly used to interface computer equipment to modems. RS-
232-C, which has extra control circuits not defined in V.24, is the *de
facto* standard used on most VDUs and printers for interfacing with
computer systems and associated data communications equipment,
but due to its similarity to V.24, only the latter will be considered
in the discussion that follows.

In V.24, the protocol elements exchanged between physical
entities are each provided by a separate circuit. The *transmit
data* and *receive data* wires, for example, provide the Data Transfer
service. In addition, flow control is implemented by the *request to
send* and *ready for sending* circuits (see Figure 4.4). Data circuits are
activated through use of the *connect data set to line, calling indicator*
and *data set ready* circuits. Quality of service parameters may be
indicated by the *data signalling rate selector* and the various *channel
signal quality* circuits. V.24 data is transmitted by representing a '1'
bit or 'OFF' by −12V, and a '0' bit or 'ON' by +12V.

X.21 and *X.21 bis* are the Physical Layer implementation standards used by the three layer CCITT X.25 recommendation for
packet-switching. X.21 and X.21 bis are themselves three layer
models (in OSI terms the Physical, Data Link and Network Layers)
but the X.25 recommendation uses only the Physical Layer of each;

this discussion is also similarly limited to the Physical Layer.

X.21 bis is used on public data networks to interface data terminal equipment to synchronous V Series modems, and is very similar to the CCITT V.24 interface. V Series modems may be used to modulate and demodulate the X.21 bis digital transmissions for use with analogue transmission media.

For speeds up to 9.6 Kbps, the 25 way D-type connector is usually used as in V.24/V.28, with −25V to −3V for a '1' bit or 'OFF' and +3V to +25V for a '0' bit or 'ON'. As with V.24, out of band signalling (that is, the use of separate circuits) is used for all control and procedural functions. For higher speeds, a 37 pin connector is used, and the data is always clocked in and out.

X.21 specifies a completely digital standard for the interface between data terminal equipment and data circuit-terminating equipment for synchronous operation on public data networks.

X.21 uses a 15 pin D-Type connector. Circuits are labelled by letters, and the procedural specification is by a transition state matrix. Transitions between states are controlled by the Control (C), Transmit Data (T), Receive Data (R) and Indication (I) circuits. For normal transmission C and I are 'ON' and data is transmitted on the T circuit and received on the R circuit.

The control signals (C and I) are available in each direction, but the standard assumes that each physical entity may transmit physical SDUs at any time, physical PDUs being transmitted by prescribed sequences of states in response to changes in the C and I circuits with steady signals on the T and R circuits.

ISDN is the international public network standard currently being defined by the CCITT. It employs wholly digital transmission techniques, and it is therefore possible to connect a user terminal to a digital telephone, and allow both voice and data traffic to share the same telephone wiring back to the exchange. The Physical Layer for ISDN is defined in CCITT recommendation I.430.

ISDN defines two logically different types of data circuit known as the 'D' channel and the 'B' channel. The 'D' channel operates

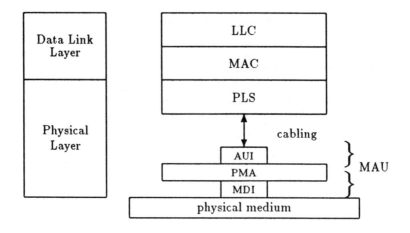

MAU — MEDIUM ATTACHMENT UNIT
LLC — LOGICAL LINK CONTROL
MAC — MEDIUM ACCESS CONTROL
PLS — PHYSICAL LEVEL SIGNALLING
AUI — ATTACHMENT UNIT INTERFACE
PMA — PHYSICAL MEDIUM ATTACHMENT
MDI — MEDIUM DEPENDENT INTERFACE

Figure 4.8 CSMA/CD sublayers in relation to the OSI model

at 16 Kbps, and the 'B' channel at 64 Kbps. Each ISDN physical connection carries two 'B' channels and a 'D' channel and is known as a '2B+D' configuration, having a net data rate of 144 Kbps full duplex. The 'B' channels provide independent end-to-end data transfer functions, and the 'D' channel provides control and signalling information for both channels, for example call set up, call clear and routeing.

Two possible implementations of the Physical Layer providing basic ISDN access are defined, both using twisted pair cables and synchronous transmission. One, the U-interface, is for two-wire connections over long distances, such as those to individual subscribers. The other, the S-interface, is for four-wire connections over short distances, intended for use in the office environment.

The *CSMA/CD* standard defined in IEEE 802.3 uses 'carrier sense multiple access and collision detection' techniques to interface with the physical medium, normally coaxial cable.   Figure 4.8 shows the relationship of CSMA/CD sublayers to the OSI model. The cabling shown in the figure is provided to allow the Medium Attachment Unit (MAU) to be some metres away from the rest of the station, thus easing installation problems for the LAN cable itself.

CSMA/CD operates in the following manner over a multiple access bus physical medium:

- when a station on the LAN wishes to transmit, it first 'listens' to the physical medium (*carrier sense*) to ascertain if any other stations are transmitting

- if the medium is not in use, it starts to transmit

- during transmission, it 'listens' to the medium to check that no other station is transmitting and corrupting its message (*collision detection*)

- if a collision is detected, it immediately stops transmitting, waits for a pseudo-random time period and tries again if the medium is free

The functions of the MAU and its constituent parts are as follows:

- the Attachment Unit Interface (AUI) provides the cabling, connectors and transmission circuitry necessary to couple the MAU and the Physical Level Signalling (PLS)

- the Physical Medium Attachment (PMA) provides the functional circuitry which allows bit streams to be transmitted and received over the physical medium at the prescribed data rate (usually 10 Mbps), together with collision detection, self test and medium test facilities

- the Medium Dependent Interface (MDI) provides the electrical and mechanical interface between the MAU and the physical medium, allowing the MAU to drive a single cable without repeater units

The maximum length of, for example, an Ethernet cable which may be driven by the MAU is 500 metres, but this may be increased by the use of repeaters which perform the OSI Physical Layer function of relaying.

The MAU may operate in normal mode, or (optionally) in monitor mode which logically disconnects it from the physical medium. Thus in OSI terms, when a data link entity requests data transfer, the physical entity (which encompasses the MAU) causes the MAU to change from monitor mode to normal mode. When it is ready, the MAU issues a *MauAvailable message*, which is used by the PLS part of the Physical Layer as a 'go ahead' for data transmission. When data transfer is complete, the opposite sequence would occur, and the MAU would return to monitor mode.

Physical SDUs are used to transmit data in the normal manner — that is, data is transferred between the Data Link Layer and the Physical Layer as individual bits. Quality of service parameters are provided by the *SignalQualityError message* which is used to detect collisions. When a collision occurs, the equivalent of the provider-initiated Reset service is used to reactivate the data circuit.

Token Ring and *Token Bus* are defined in the IEEE 802.5 and IEEE 802.4 LAN standards respectively, and have corresponding ISO standards. The former uses the ring topology, as illustrated in Figure 4.3, and the latter the bus topology of Figure 4.1. Token Ring typically transmits over shielded twisted pair cable at bit rates of 1 to 4 Mbps, or over optical fibre at bit rates up to 50 Mbps. Token Bus may use coaxial or shielded twisted pair cable (optical fibre is unsuitable for use with bus topologies). They both control access to the transmission medium by means of a sequence of control bits in the data stream called a *token*, which is passed from one station to another. A station may transmit only when it is in possession of the token. The token is 24 bits in length.

For the Token Ring, each link between two stations can be considered as a half duplex point-to-point link, since each station receives signals from the link to one of its neighbouring stations, and decodes them. If the decoded data is not addressed to that station, it re-transmits the data unchanged to its other neighbouring station. Thus data flows only in one direction around the ring. The token circulates around the ring and when a station receives a token it may insert any data it wishes to send before the token in the data stream, and then transmit the entire stream. The maximum amount of data which may be transmitted is limited by the length of time for which a station may hold the token. When a station is powered down, relays within its MAU cause a circuit to be made which closes the gap in the physical medium. The time taken for a message to reach its destination is therefore variable, depending on the number of active stations in the ring. In order to prevent corruption of the data stream, an active station is allocated the task of monitoring the ring, and maintaining a *minimum latency time* — that is, the time measured in bits for a signal to travel once around the ring. This time should be at least as long as a token, otherwise the token will become corrupted by itself as it circulates around an idle ring.

For the Token Bus, the token is passed from one station to another in a fixed sequence which is a logical ring. Again a station wishing to transmit may only do so when it is in possession of the token. However, there is no requirement for each station on the network to regenerate the circulating data stream as it passes through that node. Instead, the data stream is broadcast by the sender to all stations, and the addressee removes it from the bus as required. There is thus a deterministic delay between a station sending a message, and the receiver decoding it, which depends only on the distance of the sender from the receiver, and on the processing delay in each station. This known delay is essential for real-time control activities such as automated manufacturing.

For both these technologies, the partitioning into Data Link and Physical Layer functions is similar to that employed in CSMA/CD, with the MAC and PLS sublayers performing access control and transmitting and receiving data, and the Trunk Control Unit (TCU), similar to the MAU, providing the interface with the physical medium.

The previous paragraphs have illustrated the diversity of existing Physical Layer implementations. Since almost all of these are in widespread use and already have established standards, in order to accommodate all of them the OSI definition of the Physical Layer is of necessity lacking in detail. Further work will be done on the OSI Physical Layer, particularly on physical media connections.

5 Data Link Layer – Layer 2

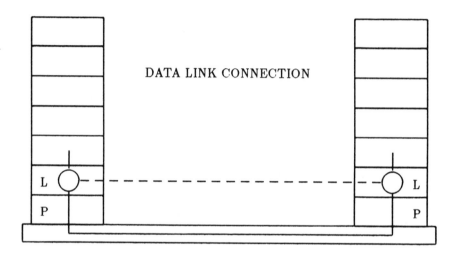

DATA LINK CONNECTION

The Data Link Layer (sometimes abbreviated to Link Layer) provides transparent transfer of data link service data units between network entities. The Physical Layer described in the previous chapter provides transparent transmission of physical service data units between data link entities. Physical service data units consist of one bit in serial transmission or n bits in parallel transmission. In the Data Link Layer the service data unit is an arbitrary but variable number of bits, containing user data and protocol information from the layers above.

The main reason for the existence of the Data Link Layer is that the data transfer service provided by the Physical Layer is often not ideal. Bits become corrupted or lost altogether during transmission, and since the Physical Layer has no knowledge of the contents of the bit stream which it is transferring, these deficiencies must be compensated for elsewhere. The Data Link Layer is the lowest at which data is manipulated before and after being transmitted over the physical medium, and it is therefore able to control the contents of the bit stream before transmission, and check them afterwards. A major requirement of the Data Link Layer is to provide transfer of data link service data units between network entities in sequence, and without corruption as far as possible. In order to provide this service, it adds extra information to the service data units before they are transmitted, which can be used to check their contents on arrival and then removed again. If corruptions do occur, the Data Link Layer can request retransmission of the data until it arrives correctly, or until it deems the physical connection to have failed in some way.

One simple analogy which can be used here is that of communicating by exchanging information through the postal system. Every letter or parcel sent by post is wrapped up, to prevent the contents from becoming separated or damaged during transit, and labelled with a destination address. Commonly, the sender's address is also added, in case the letter cannot be delivered or, in the case of business mail, to inform the recipient what is likely to be inside so that it can be directed to the correct department efficiently. There is a limit to the size of letter or parcel accepted by the Post Office for each type of service, so it may be necessary to divide the information up into smaller units before sending it. The contents of these items of mail correspond to data link service data units, their envelopes to framing information, and their addresses to data link protocol information.

It is possible for mail to become lost in the post, either permanently or just for a few days, perhaps through mis-sorting, particularly if the address is unclear, incomplete or damaged. It may therefore be necessary for the sender to number the items posted, so that the recipient can process them in the correct order, or request re-sending of missing items. The postal system itself may provide some protection against losing mail, in the form of recorded delivery or registered post. In Data Link Layer terms, the system is providing data link connections and error notification, and the user is providing sequencing of data link service data units.

There is one further aspect of the postal system which has a parallel with a Data Link Layer service, and this is the provision of the various 'classes' of mail, such as First and Second Class letter and parcel post, amongst others. This is equivalent to the Data Link Layer's provision of a selectable quality of service.

It should be emphasised that this Post Office analogy corresponds very well with the *connectionless* model for data communications. For the *connection-oriented* model, the familiar telephone network analogy can be used. Here, a connection between two parties is provided by the telephone system for the duration of the call, and the Layer 2 role of the system is to ensure that each spoken word arrives at its recipient in the correct order, preferably without being corrupted by noise. Other functions similar to those required in the Data Link Layer are implemented by the users as they conduct their conversations, punctuating their words into sentences, perhaps speaking more slowly over bad lines, asking for repetition if necessary, and so on.

If connection-oriented data transfer is to take place between network entities, a data link connection must first be established, and then released after the transfer has taken place. If the data transfer is to be connectionless as in the postal system analogy illustrated above, the Data Link Layer does not need confirmation that the remote end is ready before sending data units, and the data link connection does not really exist. For the remainder of this chapter, the emphasis will be on the connection-oriented data transfer.

5.1 Requirements for Layer 2

The purpose of the Data Link Layer is to provide transparent data transfer between two network entities, and to maintain as far as possible the integrity of the data. It must also allow the Network Layer to control the interconnection of data circuits in the Physical Layer.

To fulfil these requirements, the following services are provided to the Network Layer:

- data link connections — one or more of these may be provided between two network entities, over which data may be exchanged. A data link connection is built upon one or more physical connections

- data link service data units (LSDUs) — these contain the data exchanged by the network entities

- data link connection endpoint identifiers — if the network entities are using more than one data link connection to communicate, they may need to identify each connection separately

- sequencing — LSDUs may need to be delivered in the correct order

- error notification — if unrecoverable errors occur in the Physical Layer, they should be reported to the Network Layer

- flow control — each network entity can control the rate at which it receives LSDUs, and this may affect the rate at which the Data Link Layer will accept LSDUs from the remote data link entity

- quality of service parameters — these parameters relate to the performance characteristics of the physical connections. The Data Link Layer may be able to use physical connections of various qualities, and the qualities available should be selectable by the Network Layer. The Data Link Layer maintains the same quality of service for the entire duration of a data link connection

The provisions of the OSI reference model for Layer 2 also outline a number of functions which should be performed within the layer. These functions are described here in general terms, with specific examples given in section 5.3. Many of the functions are directly related to the services described above, but in addition the following are required:

- delimiting and synchronization — sometimes referred to as framing

- error detection and recovery — errors may be detected in the received data as a result of failures in the physical connection, or because the remote data link entity functions incorrectly: errors should be corrected by the Data Link Layer as far as possible, and only unrecoverable errors should be reported

- data circuit interconnection control — this is a transparent function which allows the Network Layer to control the inter-connection of data circuits within the Physical Layer, provided

here in Layer 2 only to maintain the consistency of the OSI
model

- data link connection splitting — one data link connection may
be split onto several physical connections in order to provide a
particular quality of service

Much of the basis for design of Data Link Layer implementations
has been the need to provide for error detection and correction
(EDC), particularly where the Physical Layer is prone to bit corruptions. This applies especially to telephone circuits, which as seen
in Chapter 1 formed the basis for many early data communications
networks. Other technologies such as optical fibre transmission
systems have very different error performance, and the Data Link
Layer requirements for EDC therefore vary. The overhead in
providing extensive EDC in a system can reduce its efficiency, and it
should only be implemented in accordance with the overall system
requirements for end-to-end error performance. If every physical
connection had a perfect transmission performance, much of the Data
Link Layer would be redundant.

Other influencing factors in the design of Data Link Layer procedures have been the desirability of sharing one physical connection
with a high rate of data transfer among many low speed data link
connections (multiplexing), and the possibility for splitting a high
speed data link connection onto a number of lower speed physical
connections. For many networks, only single channel, point-to-point
links are needed, and again some of the functionality provided by the
Data Link Layer is unnecessary.

5.2   Specification of Layer 2

Services provided to the Network Layer by the Data Link Layer
are categorised into a number of different types. The three most
commonly used types are connection-oriented, connectionless and
acknowledged connectionless. The first two categories apply to those
types of data transfer which have been discussed already, while the
third type allows for confirmation of delivery, or indication of failure
to deliver, after a connectionless transmission. A fourth type of
service is used in polled systems, where a 'master' may request a
series of 'slaves' to transmit data link information in turn.

The provision of services by the Data Link Layer is controlled by an exchange of primitives between it and the Network Layer, each primitive having a number of parameters associated with it. The services provided by the Data Link Layer fall into two categories, confirmed services and unconfirmed services. Confirmed data link services have three types of primitives associated with them: request, indication and confirm. Unconfirmed services have only the request and indication primitives.

Request primitives are passed from a network entity to the Data Link Layer to request initiation of a service. Indication primitives are passed from the Data Link Layer to the network entity to indicate an event in the Data Link Layer which is significant to the network entity. These events may be internally generated, or as a result of a remote service request. Confirm primitives are passed from the Data Link Layer to the network entity to convey the results of one or more associated previous service requests. The result may be a failure to comply, success or a degree of success.

The connectionless service requires only the Unacknowledged Connectionless Data Transfer service. This uses only L-DATA request and indication primitives, which request and indicate transfer of an LSDU. For an acknowledged connectionless service, a confirm primitive would also be associated with the data transfer. Figure 5.1 shows the primitives for the connection-oriented services, and their associated parameters. The type of service is also indicated (C — confirmed, U — unconfirmed).

The parameters used are defined as follows :

- local address — specifies the local data link service access point (LSAP) used by the data link connection
- remote address — specifies the remote LSAP together with the identifier of the remote data link entity
- LSDU — specifies the LSDU which is to be transferred or which has been received
- service class — specifies the priority required or achieved for the data unit transfer
- status — indicates success, or provides reason for failure in providing the requested service

SERVICE	PRIMITIVE	PARAMETERS	TYPE
CONNECTION ESTABLISHMENT	L-CONNECT	LOCAL ADDRESS REMOTE ADDRESS STATUS SERVICE CLASS	C
DATA TRANSFER	L-DATA-CONNECT	LOCAL ADDRESS REMOTE ADDRESS LSDU STATUS	C
CONNECTION TERMINATION	L-DISCONNECT	LOCAL ADDRESS REMOTE ADDRESS STATUS REASON	C
CONNECTION RESET	L-RESET	LOCAL ADDRESS REMOTE ADDRESS STATUS REASON	C
CONNECTION FLOW CONTROL	L-CONNECTION-FLOWCONTROL	LOCAL ADDRESS REMOTE ADDRESS AMOUNT	U

Figure 5.1 Connection-oriented Data Link Layer primitives

- amount — specifies the amount of data which may be passed between the two layers during a data transfer subject to flow control
- reason — specifies the reason for indication of a reset or disconnection

Some of the required Data Link Layer services discussed in the previous section are thus provided by using specific sets of primitives, and others are embedded services provided by the parameters of other service primitives; for example, error notification is provided by the status parameter.

The definition of Data Link Layer services in terms of primitives is only concerned with which services are provided, and not with how the provision is to be made. Once a service has been initiated by the passing of a request primitive to the Data Link Layer, the layer must perform some functions. In OSI terms, the layer entities at the local and remote nodes must exchange a predefined sequence of data link protocol data units (LPDUs) which enable them to cooperate in providing the service, and to generate the indication and confirm primitives associated with the service. As explained in Chapter 3, a protocol data unit is built up from service data units and protocol control information; in this case each LPDU is built from a maximum of one LSDU and the control information needed by the cooperating data link entities to manage the exchange and provide the service.

Figure 5.2 illustrates the exchange of primitives and LPDUs which must take place to provide the Connection-Oriented Data Transfer service. The network and data link entities are labelled 'NE' and 'LE' respectively. Note that the actual data transfer takes place via the Physical Layer.

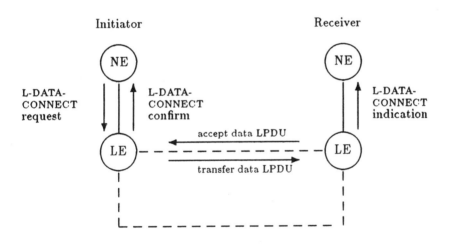

Figure 5.2 Connection-oriented transfer of data

The formulation of the data link protocol data units and their interpretation are the major tasks performed within the layer, but the method used to formulate and interpret protocol data units and the protocols themselves are outside the scope of the OSI layer standards. However, the functions which must be performed within the layer are included in the OSI definition.

Many of the concepts and terms used in practice to specify Data

Link Layer functions come, not from the OSI model, but from already existing and well-used implementation standards, which are also likely to form the basis of future Data Link Layer implementations. Before coming to a description of these established standards in section 5.3, it is appropriate to discuss the following concepts and consider them in relation to the OSI model:

- commands and responses
- procedures and elements of procedures
- timeout errors
- data link configurations
- modes of data link operation
- classes of procedure

Commands and responses — commands are LPDUs used by the initiator of a service to request the remote data link entity to take some action. Responses are LPDUs used by the recipient to acknowledge receipt of a command, to provide confirmation that action has been taken as a result of a command, to request further commands be sent to assist in the provision of a service, or to volunteer information relevant to a service being provided at the time.

Procedures — a procedure is the sequence of LPDUs exchanged by the cooperating data link entities, together with the actions which each must take during this exchange, to provide a particular service. A command and the action taken on receipt of that command are together termed an *element* of a procedure. Such an element may also include the generation of a response and the response itself.

Timeout errors — when data link entities are executing a procedure by exchanging LPDUs, it is desirable to set a limit on the length of time taken by each to respond to a command, both to maximise the use of the physical connection by eliminating long gaps in transmission, and to provide some way of detecting when a command has failed to arrive at its destination, or when a receiving station has failed to interpret the command correctly. If responses are not elicited within a period of time defined for each element of the procedure, a timeout error is said to have occurred. Timeout errors may be handled in a number of ways, for example by retransmitting the command or by resetting the link.

Data link configurations — a number of different types of data link configuration must be supported. These different configurations allow both networks which consist of a mixture of intelligent systems and unintelligent terminals, and those consisting entirely of intelligent systems, to be built within the OSI framework. For example, networks consisting of centralised switching systems and associated terminals, analogous to telephone exchanges and telephones, are provided for, as are those in which every network user can perform control and routeing functions. These different types of system are distinguished using the terms *primary*, *secondary* and *combined stations*.

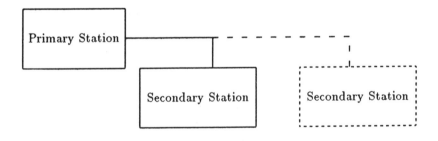

Figure 5.3 Unbalanced data link configuration

A primary data station is the Data Link Layer of a node which can formulate and send command LPDUs, receive responses, and which is responsible for data link error recovery and data link management. A secondary station is the Data Link Layer of a node which can only accept commands, send responses and initiate data link error recovery. If a primary and a secondary station are coupled, the resulting configuration is termed *unbalanced* (see Figure 5.3). More than one secondary station can be coupled to the same primary station.

The third class of station is that of combined stations, which can perform the functions of both the primary and the secondary stations. When two combined stations are coupled, they share responsibility for the data link, and the resulting configuration is termed *balanced* (see Figure 5.4). Two unbalanced data links may also be operated in opposite directions over one data circuit. This configuration is termed *symmetrical* (Figure 5.5).

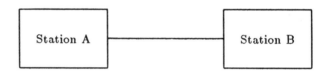

Figure 5.4 Balanced data link configuration

Examples of unbalanced system configurations are terminals connected to computers through data switches and the proposed ISDNs, where terminals are connected to Integrated Services PBXs or public exchanges. Typical balanced systems are the CSMA/CD and Token Ring based LANs, where every station is a combined one.

Modes — as well as providing for different data link configurations, the Data Link Layer allows the links to be operated in different modes. A mode may be operational or non-operational, and a primary or combined station may change the mode of the link by sending mode setting command LPDUs. Once a mode has been established, only a predefined set of procedures may be used by each station on the link, until a mode setting command is issued which changes the current mode.

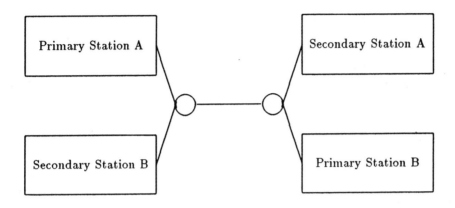

Figure 5.5 Symmetrical data link configuration

An operational data link may be in either *asynchronous* or *normal* response mode. Normal response mode (NRM) applies to unbalanced data links, and allows the secondary station to transmit only when explicitly given permission to do so by the primary station. Asynchronous modes can be used by both unbalanced and balanced data links, giving rise to the asynchronous unbalanced response mode (ARM) and the asynchronous balanced response mode (ABM). In ARM the secondary station can transmit response LPDUs without explicit permission from the primary station if it detects an idle condition on the data link, and in ABM the combined stations can both initiate transmissions at any time of both command and response LPDUs.

A non-operational data link may be in either *disconnected* or *initialisation* mode. The disconnected modes are normal disconnected mode (NDM) and asynchronous disconnected mode (ADM). When a station is in a disconnected mode, it cannot transmit or accept LPDUs from the link, but it can take action on command LPDUs which change the mode, and respond with a fixed set of responses to polls. (A 'poll' is a type of command which means "Are you there?") In ADM, a station may give such a response whenever it detects an idle link condition, or if it is a combined station it may also issue a mode change command, whereas in NDM it may only respond when explicitly told to do so.

A secondary or combined station may be placed in initialisation mode (IM) by the primary or other combined station when it appears to be operating abnormally, or when it requests initialisation itself. In IM, the two stations exchange a predefined sequence of LPDUs until a mode setting command is acknowledged by the secondary or combined station, or until it fails and becomes disconnected.

Classes of procedure — in order to support each of the various modes of operation, only a subset of all the procedures which are defined within the Data Link Layer is required. For any mode, a class of procedures can be defined which restricts the cooperating stations to using only those procedures required to operate a data link in that mode. The provision of these subsets of functions within the Data Link Layer serves to minimise the implementation and processing overhead for each piece of equipment. Each class of procedures allows only a subset of the possible command and response LPDUs to be used. A primary station may use only the subset of commands, and a secondary station may use only the subset of responses. A combined station may use both.

This section has been concerned mainly with the classification and implementation of the protocols between data link entities. Another group of concepts and terms is associated with delimiting of LPDUs within the transmitted bit stream, sequencing of LSDUs and error detection. These functions all involve manipulating data at the interface between the Data Link and Physical Layers. Since the Physical Layer may only transmit and receive bit streams without modifying them, all the manipulation must be performed within the Data Link Layer. The concepts and terms to be discussed here are:

- frames and framing

- numbered and unnumbered frames

- frame check sequences

Frames — the Data Link Layer is the lowest at which data can be manipulated prior to transmission; therefore the sequence of bits transferred to the Physical Layer must contain all the information required to perform all the functions of the Data Link Layer, as well as of the layers above. Chapter 3 illustrated how a core of data is passed from layer to layer, and how each layer adds its own protocol control information (PCI) to the core. The Data Link Layer is no different. Core data LSDUs are passed between the Data Link Layer and the Network Layer, together with associated interface control information (ICI). The data link entities extract the LSDUs and add their own PCI to create LPDUs.

However, the Data Link Layer is also required to provide delimiting so that an LPDU can be extracted from a continuous stream of bits which is being received over the physical connection. This bit stream may contain LPDUs from a number of different sources, either contiguously or separated by idle periods. Before an LPDU can be interpreted by the Data Link Layer, it must first be delimited within the bit stream, and then recognised as being destined for this data link connection endpoint. In order to provide these functions, it is common for the Data Link Layer to add a further unique pattern of bits at the start (and sometimes also the end) of each LPDU, and to guarantee the pattern's uniqueness by adjusting the contents of the LPDU accordingly. This process, and the associated process of recognising the unique pattern, removing it and compensating for any adjustment, is called *framing*, and the actual sequence of bits transferred to the Physical Layer by the Data Link Layer is called a frame.

Numbered and unnumbered frames — in order to provide sequencing of LSDUs for the Network Layer, the Data Link Layer needs to label LPDUs so that if one is lost during transmission, or arrives out of order, this can be detected and corrected for by requesting a retransmission or by re-sequencing LSDUs within the layer. This sequencing is normally performed by numbering the LPDUs, and checking the numbers of received LPDUs against the expected number.

Some LPDUs may only be exchanged between the data link entities during the establishment and release of a data link connection, or for testing or initialisation purposes. Such LPDUs may not contain any information which originates outside the Data Link Layer — that is, there is no associated LSDU and there is no need to provide any sequencing other than that governed by the relevant procedures. These LPDUs do not need to be numbered. Frames which contain numbered LPDUs are termed numbered frames, and those that do not are termed unnumbered. Unnumbered frames may also be used when there is no requirement to take measures to guarantee sequence integrity, for example on an error-free, point-to-point link. In this case the LPDUs may or may not contain LSDUs.

Frame check sequences (FCS) — once an LPDU has been prepared by the Data Link Layer and its contents in terms of actual bits to be transmitted are known, some error detection information can be added to it. This information normally takes the form of extra bits added before the end marker of a frame, and these bits are a result of performing some logical combination of the other bits within the frame, such as a modulo-16 addition of groups of 16 bits to form a 16 bit result. When the frame is received and the start and end markers have been removed, the logical combination can be performed again, and the result checked against the last 16 bits received. These groups of bits are therefore called frame check sequences.

The preceding discussions have indicated some key areas which must be considered when specifying a particular Data Link Layer implementation. Different data communications networks have varying requirements for data link configurations, modes of operation, error detection, sequencing and so on, depending on the network topology, characteristics of the physical connections and the services required by higher layers.

It should be noted that some of the functions allowed for at Layer 2 may be provided by higher layers — for example, sequence integrity and error detection. Also, provision of connection-oriented services may be performed at a higher layer, based only on the connectionless services of the Data Link Layer.

5.3   Discussion of Technologies

Most current implementations of the Data Link Layer are based on the ISO standard *High-level data link control (HDLC) procedures* (Reference 5.1). Examples of these implementations include:

- the Data Link Layer of the CCITT X.25 recommendation for public packet-switched networks, termed LAP-B
- the ISDN D-channel access, termed LAP-D
- the IEEE 802 Series of recommendations for LANs, adopted by ISO
- IBM's proprietary Layer 2 equivalent for its SNA products, called SDLC (Synchronous Data Link Control)

As it has obvious relevance to the definition of the OSI Data Link Layer, a summary of HDLC will be provided here, but for the details the reader should consult Reference 5.1.

The HDLC standard defines:

- the frame structure used to transfer control information and data
- the bit patterns used to encode each command and response
- the method of assembling and disassembling frames to guarantee the uniqueness of the start and end patterns of bits
- the elements of procedures
- a number of classes of procedure

The HDLC frame consists of the components shown in Figure 5.6. Each frame is delimited at the start and end by a *flag*. After the flag comes addressing information followed by an indication of the frame type, and control information. Data for transparent transfer may then be optionally included, and finally a frame check sequence (FCS) is added.

The basic HDLC format assumes a maximum of one primary station at each end of a physical connection, but when the physical connection has a multipoint architecture, and all stations are capable

| Flag | Address | Control | Information | FCS | Flag |

Figure 5.6 HDLC frame format

of operating as primary stations, a source address must be included in the frame together with the destination address.

An HDLC flag is one *octet* (eight bits) in length. The address and control fields are a single octet long normally, but may be extended. The information field consists of zero or more octets and the FCS is two or four octets. Note that a single flag may be used to perform both the closing function for one frame and the opening function for the succeeding frame. The octets in the frame shown in Figure 5.6 are always transmitted in sequence, from left to right as illustrated. Within an octet, the lowest order bit is transmitted first.

The HDLC flag has the bit pattern 01111110, that is a zero followed by six ones followed by a zero. In order to allow transparency, confusion of the flag octet with data octets must be prevented; this is done using a technique called zero-bit insertion (sometimes called 'bit-stuffing'). As the flag contains a sequence of six '1' bits, all data to be transmitted is scanned for sequences of five consecutive '1' bits, and if this is found the Data Link Layer inserts a '0' bit after the fifth '1' bit; the receiver scans the input stream for sequences of five '1' bits and removes the following '0' bit after testing for flags (zero-bit removal).

The address field is used to identify the different stations on a link. For a point-to-point link this is redundant information, but in multipoint links it is essential. In a command frame, the address identifies the station(s) for which the command is intended. In a response frame, it identifies the responder. Two addresses are reserved by HDLC. The address field pattern 11111111 is defined as the all-station address, used for broadcast commands, and the pattern 00000000 is the no-station address used for test purposes.

In normal addressing a single octet may be used to identify up to 256 addresses. By prior agreement by both ends of the data link, more than one octet may be used. This is called extended addressing. If this is used then the low order bit is set to zero to indicate that the next octet also contains address information; this may be repeated, the address extension ceasing when an address octet is received with the low order bit set to one — note that in this case only seven bits per octet may be used for addressing.

There is no specification for the format of the information field. It may contain an unspecified number of bits in any sequence. This is a good example of the 'black box' nature of each OSI layer, since the Data Link Layer knows nothing of the contents of the information field, and does not need to do so in order to carry out its functions.

The FCS is generated by polynomial arithmetic on the bits between the flags. Polynomial arithmetic is used because it allows the FCS to be generated at the sending end, and checked at the receiving end, by bit serial arithmetic — that is, the serial bit stream is processed on a bit by bit basis. The results of the arithmetic on the bits in the address, control and information fields are added to the bit stream before the closing flag at the sending end. These results are the FCS, and may be 16 or 32 bits long. The receiver performs the same polynomial arithmetic on all the bits between the flags, including the FCS, and the result should always be a constant known value. For the details of this arithmetic, and the polynomials used, the reader should consult Reference 5.1. It should be noted that the FCS is generated before zero-bit insertion at the sending end, and after zero-bit removal at the receiving end.

Between frames, an *inter-frame time fill* is specified. This may be either contiguous flags, or between seven and fourteen contiguous '1' bits or a combination of the two, depending on other system requirements. A frame is invalid if it is less than 32 bits long between flags for the 16 bit FCS format, or less than 48 bits for the 32 bit FCS format, or if it is not properly enclosed by flags. If a frame is invalid it is discarded, so if a frame ends with seven or more contiguous '1' bits it will be ignored since this signifies inter-frame time fill. Similarly, a frame cannot be closed until a flag has been properly received.

Type of Frame Format	Control Field Bits							
	1	2	3	4	5	6	7	8
I Frame Format	0	N(S)			P/F	N(R)		
S Frame Format	1	0	S	S	P/F	N(R)		
U Frame Format	1	1	M	M	P/F	M	M	M

Figure 5.7 HDLC control fields

The HDLC commands and responses are encoded into the control field of a frame. There are three basic frame types, each having a different format. The format for normal control field mode is as shown in Figure 5.7. In extended control field mode, 16 bits are used, and the N(R) and N(S) fields each use seven bits. The use of the three types of frame format is as follows:

- *I frame* format is used to perform information transfer

- *S frame* format is used to supervise the data link. It can be used to suspend and restart the transmission of I frames in addition to requesting the transmission and retransmission (after errors) of I frames

- *U frame* format is used to send unnumbered frames and provides additional data link control

The usage of the individual control field bits is described in the following paragraphs.

N(S) is the *send sequence number* used to identify the sequence number of each transmitted I frame. Sequence numbers are 0 to 7 for eight bit control fields and 0 to 127 for extended control fields. Prior to transmitting each frame, N(S) is incremented modulo-8 or modulo-128 from the previous value sent.

N(R) is the *receive sequence number* used in I and S frames to indicate the N(S) of the next expected frame, thereby indicating to the sender that frames up to N(R)–1 have been successfully received.

P/F is the *poll/final* bit and performs two functions:

- in a command frame it is a poll or P bit, which when set to '1' is an invitation for the secondary station to transmit one or more responses
- in a response frame it is a final or F bit and has the following meanings:
  - if '0' it indicates that the response is continued in a subsequent frame
  - if '1' it indicates that this is the final frame of the response

If a command frame is received with the P bit set, the secondary station can acknowledge the receipt by responding with a frame with the F bit set. The P and F bits always operate in pairs, therefore a primary station will not transmit another P bit until the corresponding F bit has been sent back, nor will the secondary station ever transmit an F bit without receiving a P bit.

The S bits are the *S frame command or response* bits. These two bits can take four different meanings, as shown in Figure 5.8. The meaning of each of these values is as follows:

- *RR* invites the transmission of I frames and acknowledges previous frames up to N(R)–1 inclusive
- *REJ* requests the retransmission of all frames numbered N(R) and subsequent, and acknowledges previous frames up to N(R)–1 inclusive
- *RNR* is used to indicate a station is temporarily busy, and acknowledges previous frames up to N(R)–1 inclusive. Any frames received after transmission of RNR should be dealt with in subsequent frames

S Bits	Mnemonic	Command
00	RR	Receive Ready
01	REJ	Reject
10	RNR	Receive Not Ready
11	SREJ	Selective Reject

Figure 5.8 S Frame commands and responses

- *SREJ* is used to request the retransmission of frame N(R) and acknowledges previous frames up to N(R)–1 inclusive. Frames transmitted after N(R) should not be retransmitted unless subsequently requested by a further REJ or SREJ — neither of which should be transmitted until the response to the original SREJ has been received

M indicates the five M bits of the unnumbered format control frames. They can take the different meanings shown in Figures 5.9 and 5.10: the former illustrates the M bit patterns used for command frames, and the latter those used for response frames. The usage of the various patterns is as follows:

- *Mode setting* commands fall into two categories. SNRM, SARM, SABM, SNRME, SARME and SABME are used to establish a mode of operation, as discussed in section 5.2. The extended modes use the two octet option for the control field, which allows N(R) and N(S) to operate modulo-128, instead of modulo-8 as in the one octet control field modes. DISC, RSET and SIM are used for setting non-operational modes. These commands are all acknowledged by a UA response

- *UP* is acknowledged by the transmission of response frames from the stations specified by the group identified by the

M Bits	Mnemonic	Command
00 001	SNRM	Set Normal Response Mode
11 000	SARM	Set Asynchronous Response Mode
11 100	SABM	Set Asynchronous Balanced Mode
00 010	DISC	Disconnect
11 011	SNRME	Set Normal Response Mode Extended
11 010	SARME	Set Asynchronous Response Mode Extended
11 110	SABME	Set Asynchronous Balanced Mode Extended
10 000	SIM	Set Initialisation Mode
00 100	UP	Unnumbered Poll
00 000	UI	Unnumbered Information
11 101	XID	Exchange Identification
11 001	RSET	Reset
00 111	TEST	Test

Figure 5.9 Unnumbered command frames

M Bits	Mnemonic	Command
00 110	UA	Unnumbered Acknowledge
10 001	FRMR	Frame Reject
11 000	DM	Disconnect Mode
00 010	RD	Request Disconnect
10 000	RIM	Request Initialisation Mode
00 000	UI	Unnumbered Information
11 101	XID	Exchange Identification
00 111	TEST	Test

Figure 5.10 Unnumbered responses

address field. Response is mandatory if the UP frame has the P bit set, otherwise optional

- *UI* frames are undefined and are used to transmit information without incrementing N(R) and N(S). It is not mandatory to acknowledge UI frames

- *XID* frames are used to collect information about the stations on the data link, and are acknowledged by a responding XID frame giving details of the addressed station

- *TEST* frames are acknowledged using an identical TEST frame and cause no change of N(R) or N(S)

- *UA* acknowledges an unnumbered command

- *FRMR* rejects a frame. Retransmission of the frame would not cure the problem as the recipient is unable to action the command

PROCEDURE CLASS	COMMANDS	RESPONSES
UNC	I	I
	RR	RR
	RNR	RNR
	SARM	UA
	DISC	DM
		FRMR
UAC	I	I
	RR	RR
	RNR	RNR
	SARM	UA
	DISC	DM
		FRMR
BAC	I	I
	RR	RR
	RNR	RNR
	SABM	UA
	DISC	DM
		FRMR

Figure 5.11 Fundamental repertoires of HDLC classes of procedure

- *DM* reports that the station is logically disconnected from the link

- *RD* reports that the station requires to be disconnected from the link, and requests a DISC command. If any frames are acknowledged after transmission of RD, the primary station ignores the RD

- *RIM* requests a re-initialisation command (SIM). RIM may be retransmitted whilst awaiting the SIM command

Three fundamental classes of procedure are defined by the HDLC standard: unbalanced operation normal response mode class (UNC), unbalanced operation asynchronous response mode class (UAC), and balanced operation asynchronous response mode class (BAC). The basic compulsory repertoires for commands and responses are shown in Figure 5.11. A number of options are also permitted, which include the addition of the commands XID, REJ, SREJ, UI, UP, RSET (BAC only), TEST, together with their appropriate responses and the RD response. The extended control field mode commands may also be used (for example, SARME would replace SARM), the 32 bit FCS option may be used instead of the 16 bit option, and extended

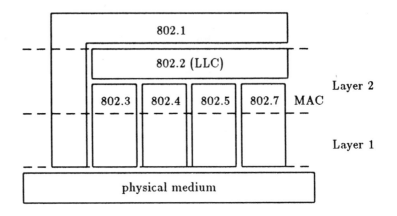

Figure 5.12 IEEE 802 inter-relationships

addressing may also be used.

As stated at the beginning of this section, subsets of HDLC procedures are used by many existing implementation standards. The CCITT X.25 recommendation uses a Layer 2 protocol which it terms a Link Access Protocol (LAP). The current recommendations use the BAC class of procedures of HDLC, but earlier networks implemented an earlier version of the protocol which predated the ISO definition of HDLC. These two versions are called LAP-B and LAP respectively. Only LAP-B will be offered by all networks in the future.

The IEEE 802 Series LAN standards also use the HDLC BAC class of procedures, but the functions of HDLC are split between two sublayers: the Logical Link Control sublayer (LLC) and the Medium Access Control sublayer (MAC). The structure of this partitioning and the inter-relationship of the various members of the

PRIMITIVE	PARAMETERS
MA-DATA.request	DESTINATION ADDRESS MSDU REQUESTED SERVICE CLASS
MA-DATA.indication	DESTINATION ADDRESS SOURCE ADDRESS MSDU RECEPTION STATUS REQUESTED SERVICE CLASS
MA-DATA.confirm	TRANSMISSION STATUS PROVIDED SERVICE CLASS

Figure 5.13 LLC to MAC sublayer primitives

IEEE 802 Series standards are illustrated in Figure 5.12. The MAC sublayer standards define different LAN access methods as follows:

- IEEE 802.3 — CSMA/CD bus
- IEEE 802.4 — token passing bus
- IEEE 802.5 — token passing ring
- IEEE 802.7 — slotted ring

The Layer 2 functions are separated into two classifications: those associated with the formulation and interpretation of commands and responses are performed in the Logical Link Control sublayer, and those associated with synchronization, delimiting of LPDUs (framing), error detection using FCS, and the insertion and recognition of addresses are performed by the Medium Access Control sublayer.

The LLC procedures and command/response formats for the connection-oriented mode (LLC Type 2) are derived from the HDLC BAC class of procedures, using the extended control field option. LLC Types 1 and 3 are for the connectionless and acknowledged connectionless respectively. For all types, the primitives exchanged between the Network Layer and the LLC are as specified in the OSI model. LLC PDUs are passed to the MAC, where they are formatted into MAC frames ready for transmission by the Physical Layer. The format of the MAC frame, and the procedures used for access control are different for each MAC sublayer standard, allowing variations

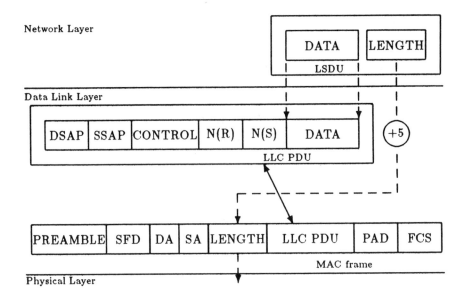

Figure 5.14 Relationship between LLC PDU and MAC frame

which are appropriate to the topology and physical medium used
by the LAN. MAC services are provided through the exchange of
sublayer primitives between it and the LLC, listed in Figure 5.13.
The relationship between LLC PDUs and MAC frames is illustrated
in Figure 5.14.

For a detailed description of these LAN implentations, and of
the other standards derived from HDLC used for Data Link Layer
implementations, the reader should consult references 5.2 to 5.8.

5.4   References

5.1 *High-level data link control (HDLC) procedures* (BS 5397, all
parts), British Standards Institution, 1985.   (This document is
equivalent to ISO 4335.)

5.2 *Logical link control for local area networks* (DD 99, all parts), British Standards Institution, 1985. (This document is equivalent to ISO/DP 8802/2 and IEEE 802.2 Draft E.)

5.3 *CSMA/CD local area networks* (ISO/DP 8802/3), International Organization for Standardization, 1984. (This document is equivalent to IEEE 802.3, and related to BSI DD 98 : 1985.)

5.4 *Token bus local area networks* (ISO/DP 8802/4), International Organization for Standardization, 1984. (This document is equivalent to IEEE 802.4 Draft F, and related to BSI DD 100 : 1985.)

5.5 *Token ring local area networks* (DD 136), British Standards Institution, 1986. (This document is equivalent to ISO/DP 8802/5 and IEEE 802.5.)

5.6 *10 Mbps slotted ring local area network* (BS 6531, all parts and BS 6532, all parts), British Standards Institution, 1984. (These documents are equivalent to ISO/DP 8802/6 and IEEE 802.7.)

5.7 'Data communications networks: interfaces. Recommendations X.20 – X.32', *Red Book*, Volume VIII, Fascicle VIII.3, International Telegraph and Telephone Consultative Committee, 1985.

5.8 'Integrated Services Digital Network (ISDN). Series I Recommendations', *Red Book*, Volume III, Fascicle III.5, International Telegraph and Telephone Consultative Committee, 1985.

6 Network Layer – Layer 3

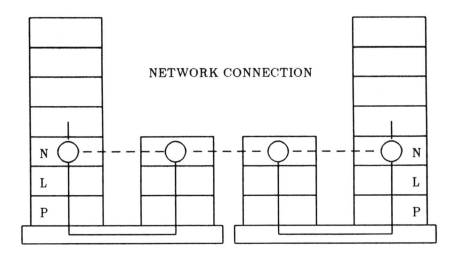

NETWORK CONNECTION

The Network Layer provides transparent transfer of data between two corresponding network service users (transport entities). The main purpose of the Network Layer is to provide routeing of network service data units (NSDUs) between network service users in communicating end open systems. Routeing may involve the use of intermediate open systems as relays, but this relaying function is invisible, both to the Transport Layer and to the layers above.

When discussing the Network Layer, it is important to distinguish between the OSI network service and that provided by a system in the real world, for example, the telephone network service. The term 'network' will be reserved here for the context of OSI, and the word 'subnetwork' will be used to describe real network systems, whether they are open or not.

Routeing is commonly termed *switching* in communications systems, because early systems could only make and break connections through use of physical switches, such as the patch panel mentioned in Chapter 1 (Figure 1.3). The mechanics of switching are actually performed in the Physical Layer of a real open system, but are directly controlled from the Network Layer. Data communications systems which are based around data PABXs route data through the control of a switching matrix, which allows any two data channels to be interconnected.

When a dedicated circuit is provided between two subnetwork service users, such that its entire bandwidth is available to them for the duration of their communication session, the routeing function is termed *circuit-switching*. Good examples of real circuit-switched networks are the PSTNs. Within a circuit-switched network, the tariffs for data traffic are usually based on the bandwidth of the circuit provided and the duration of the data call, regardless of how much data is actually transferred.

Although it may be the case that a separate physical medium is used for each circuit, normally many circuits are multiplexed together onto one high speed transmission channel, as discussed in Chapter 4. In circuit-switching, a fixed amount of bandwidth is made available to each circuit for the duration of its existence. In *packet-switching*, bandwidth is made available to corresponding subnetwork service users on a demand basis, and the tariffs for packet-switched networks are based on the amount of data actually transferred, not how long it took to transfer it.

The term 'packet' refers to the protocol data unit used at the Network Layer, and was originally chosen to distinguish it from other terms such as 'block', 'record' or 'segment', which already had particular meanings within computer systems. In OSI terms, a packet is equivalent to a network protocol data unit (NPDU), since it contains protocol information and, optionally, NSDUs. Note that the unit of data actually transmitted through the physical medium is in fact the frame created in the Data Link Layer, which contains the NPDU. In packet-switched systems, packets from many subnetwork users are interleaved by switching nodes onto high speed transmission channels in such a way as to optimise the use of the available bandwidth. An individual subnetwork user is only allocated bandwidth when it has a packet to send or receive.

For a large subnetwork having many switching nodes there may be a number of routes which data could take between any two points (see Figure 6.1). Route selection in both packet- and circuit-switched systems is normally based on such criteria as data traffic congestion, cost and quality of service. At its simplest, the selection of route may involve use of a look-up table which prioritises possible routes. Complex algorithms may also be used to optimise a route for one or more of the criteria listed above.

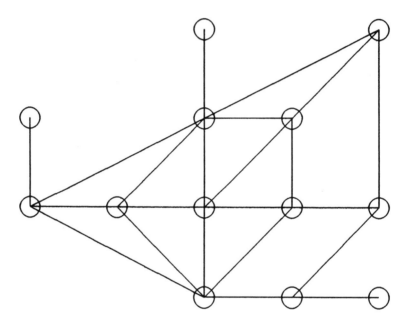

Figure 6.1 A subnetwork with many routes between nodes

Packet-switched systems may use a number of different routeing techniques. One technique is to perform routeing separately for each packet. A parallel to this is the sorting process used in the postal service for each item of mail. There is no guarantee that items posted from one place to another will arrive in order, or take the same route. Similarly, in a packet-switched system, if the route selection method permits different paths to be taken between the same pair of subnetwork users, some packets may take faster routes than others. A sequence of packets sent from one subnetwork user to another may therefore arrive out of order. There is also a considerable system overhead in providing the route selection repetitively. However, when only a small amount of data is to be transferred, it may be economical to transfer it in one packet which also contains all the protocol information required to assure its delivery.

For the case where many packets are to be exchanged between two subnetwork users, it is useful to establish an optimal route between them which will be used by all packets for the duration of their communication session. This reduces the route selection overhead to a minimum, and also enables the communications session to be conducted as a data call, similar to those used in circuit-switched systems. Since such a facility in a packet-switched system looks to the user as if a circuit is allocated, it is said to have used a *virtual circuit* and is termed a *virtual call* to distinguish it from a (real) call in a circuit-switched system. Calls, both virtual and real have a set-up phase, a data transfer phase and a call release phase. NPDUs are delivered in sequence with consistent quality throughout a call in either type of system.

As mentioned in Chapter 5, communication systems may provide either connectionless or connection-oriented services — that is, either analogous to the postal service, or to the telephone system. At the Network Layer, as at the Data Link Layer, both types of service may be provided regardless of that available from the layer below. Above the Network Layer, services may only be provided which have the same type as that provided by the Network Layer. The connection-oriented network service, or CONS as it is abbreviated, involves the provision of network connections — that is, the circuits and virtual circuits referred to above. The connectionless network service involves no network connection provision, and is implemented by the use of single packets containing all the protocol information necessary for their delivery.

Although routeing is an essential part of the network service provided by the Network Layer, there is no OSI defined routeing algorithm or method. The routeing function is part of the management function of the Network Layer, and its specification is left entirely up to the system designer. However, in the definition of Network Layer services, some provision is made for including information concerned with routeing in the Network Layer protocols. In particular, the issue of addressing is considered within this layer.

6.1   Requirements for Layer 3

The principal requirement of the Network Layer is that it should allow transparent transfer of data between network service users. The Network Layer is responsible for ensuring that data passed into it from the Transport Layer is transmitted through the communications media to the correct receiving transport entity. The structure and detailed content of the data transmitted by the Network Layer between transport entities are determined by the Transport Layer and the layers above it, and are not modified by the Network Layer.

The boundary between the Network and Transport Layers is particularly significant within the OSI model, for the Network Layer conceals from the layers above the details of the actual communication technology required to complete the connection between two open systems. The Network Layer is required to provide the Transport Layer with the quality of service which has been negotiated between the network service and transport entities at connection time. This quality of service should be provided at a known cost to the Transport Layer. Beyond these considerations of cost and quality of service, however, the Network Layer relieves the Transport Layer of all concern for the routeing and relaying of data over a real subnetwork. It should be noted that the quality of service provided by the Network Layer depends on that available from the Data Link Layer. Although some compensation is possible for errors in the Network Layer, it is assumed in its specification that the Data Link Layer provides an almost error-free data link connection.

The following specific services are provided by the Network Layer to fulfil the requirements outlined above:

- network connection establishment — to allow transport entities in end open systems to establish a connection

- normal data exchange — to allow the transfer of network service data units over the network connection and to maintain the integrity of the NSDUs in transit between the connected transport entities

- network connection release — to allow a transport entity to request the release of a network connection, with possible loss of data in transit, and also to allow a network entity to indicate to transport entities that a provider-initiated connection release has taken place

- addressing — to provide transport entities with a network address by which they can uniquely identify transport entities in other end open systems

- quality of service parameters — to establish and maintain a quality of service selected at connection time, including considerations of error rate, availability, throughput and delay, amongst others

- error notification — to inform the connected transport entities of any unrecoverable errors detected by the Network Layer

- sequencing — to provide, at the request of transport entities, sequenced delivery of NSDUs over the subnetwork

- flow control — to allow a receiving transport entity to stop transferral of NSDUs to it by the network service

In addition to the services listed above, the Network Layer may optionally provide the following:

- expedited data transfer — to allow an alternative means for transmitting data over the network connection, subject to separate flow control and network service characteristics

- reset — to allow a transport entity to cause the Network Layer to discard all NSDUs in transit and to inform the receiving transport entity that the reset has taken place

- receipt confirmation — to allow a transport entity to confirm that the NSDUs have been received

If required, these optional services must be requested by the network service user, in which case the Network Layer may either comply with the request, or inform the requesting transport entity that the service is unavailable. It should be noted that confirmation of receipt is included in the OSI Network Layer only to increase compatibility with the Layer 3 requirements contained in the CCITT X.25 packet-switching recommendation.

The Network Layer is required to provide transport entities with a network service which is consistent with the OSI standards

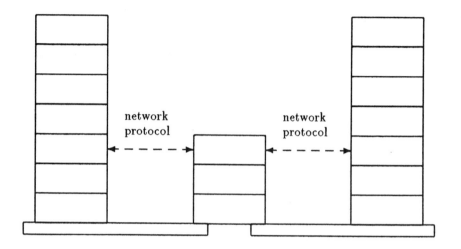

Figure 6.2 Connection using a single network protocol

for the layer. Transport entities exist only in end open systems, whereas the Network Layer commonly makes use of network entities in intermediate open systems (see Figure 3.8) which only provide the network service indirectly to network service users. Their explicit function is to act as relays between the end open systems where the connected transport entities reside. (In some situations, a particular hardware configuration implementing Layers 1, 2 and 3 may serve both as an intermediate open system and as the lower layers of an end open system.)

The Network Layer has to be sufficiently flexible in its structure to accommodate this division between end and intermediate open systems. In addition, it must be able to provide transport entities with the OSI network service even when making use of real subnetworks which do not fully support OSI. This flexibility is achieved by having more than one network protocol, to *harmonize* subnetworks with OSI. Harmonization may involve the masking of some features of subnetworks which do not comply with OSI requirements; other features may need to be enhanced if the full network service is to be maintained. Figure 6.2 shows end open

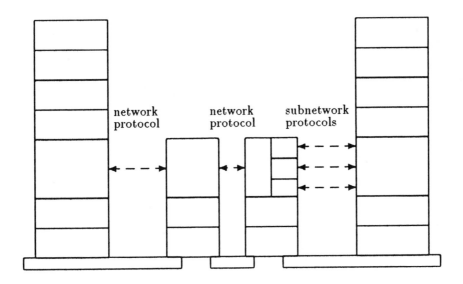

Figure 6.3 Connection using multiple protocols

systems connected over an OSI-conformant subnetwork using a single
protocol. In Figure 6.3, the end open systems are connected over two
subnetworks, one of which is not OSI-conformant. In this case, the
OSI subnetwork is connected using a single network protocol, while
the other subnetwork requires three subnetwork protocols to fulfil
the requirements of the Network Layer.

6.2   Specification of Layer 3

Before considering the specification of the detailed services which are
provided by the Network Layer, network addressing and the use of
a 'queue' model for flow control will be discussed. Familiarity with
both concepts is necessary for a full understanding of the operation
of the Network Layer.

The provision of network addresses to network service users is
a particularly important function of the Network Layer. The term
'network address' is one whose meaning tends to vary according to
context: in OSI, *network address* is an abbreviation of *network service
access point address* (NSAP address), the point on the boundary

between Layers 3 and 4 at which a network service is made available to a network service user. To avoid confusion, 'NSAP address' will be used in the discussion which follows.

NSAP addresses are provided by the Network Layer as a means of identifying transport entities, and are used by transport entities in establishing end-to-end connections between end open systems. The NSAP address has a dual function: first to identify an end open system and secondly to identify a transport entity within that open system. Network service primitives such as N-CONNECT and N-DISCONNECT include NSAP addresses amongst their parameters; the encoded NSAP address is transferred as network protocol control information and is known as *network protocol address information* (NPAI). For example, the called and calling addresses in N-CONNECT are NPAI necessary for the Network Layer to establish a connection between specified transport entities.

In the OSI environment, *addressing authorities* are responsible for allocating unambiguous NSAP addresses within their own *network addressing domain*. A network addressing domain may be a part of a higher network addressing domain, in which case the higher addressing authority authorises the lower addressing authority in its allocation of addresses. Ultimately all network addressing domains are a part of the *global network addressing domain*, which contains all the NSAP addresses within the OSI environment; the ultimate addressing authority is the OSI through its published standards (see Reference 6.6). At the lowest level, the addressing authority might be the manager of a single LAN, while at the highest levels, the CCITT and the ISO are responsible for the allocation of NSAP addresses.

The structure of the NSAP address reflects the hierarchical structure of addressing domains and authorities. An NSAP address consists of two parts, the *initial domain part* (IDP) and the *domain specific part* (DSP) (see Figure 6.4). The IDP identifies a subdomain of the global network addressing domain and its associated addressing authority; the DSP is an address within the subdomain and may be either an NSAP address or the identifier of a lower level subdomain. Taken together, the IDP and the DSP allow any NSAP address to be identified unambiguously from any other NSAP address within any OSI end system.

A distinction should be made between network addressing as

described above and routeing across real subnetworks. The addressing function of the Network Layer uses the called and calling
NSAP addresses to determine which network entities in intermediate
systems are required to make the connection between end-system
transport entities. Although NSAP addresses are known to transport
entities, they cannot derive routes from NSAP addresses.

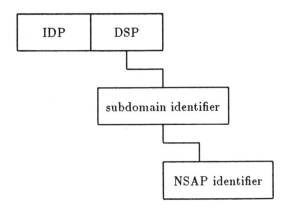

Figure 6.4 Structure of an NSAP address

In determining a route through the Network Layer, the addressing function makes use of *subnetwork point of attachment* (SNPA)
addresses. An SNPA is the point of attachment between a real
subnetwork and a piece of equipment which might be a real end
system or another real subnetwork. The relationship between
an SNPA address and an equivalent NSAP address is potentially
complex, and the processing of routeing across real subnetworks
requires use of SNPA/NSAP directories in the Network Layer.

The relationship between network service users and the network
service itself can be modelled using the concept of a *queue*, as shown

in Figure 6.5. The network connection is represented as a pair of queues between the connected NSAPs; the network service users can add objects to or remove objects from the appropriate queue, representing the flow of data between them.

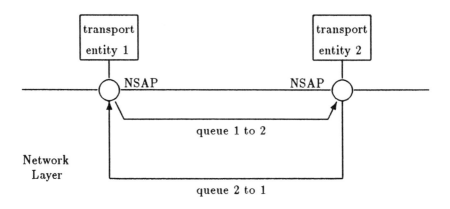

Figure 6.5 Network connection modelled as a pair of queues

The objects which travel along the queue are, amongst others, octets of user data, expedited NSDUs and data relating to the connection establishment and release primitives. The entities providing the network connection can themselves add a limited group of objects to the queue, in particular those associated with the provider-initiated reset and disconnect functions of the Network Layer.

The queue has an undefined but limited capacity, with the receiving network service user alone able to remove objects from it. The consequence is that *flow control* between transport entities is achieved by managing the capacity of the queue and by defining the relationship between different types of object in the queue. For example, the addition of an object of user data may prevent addition of further user data, but will not prevent the addition of an expedited

PRIMITIVE	PARAMETERS	TYPE
N-CONNECT	CALLED ADDRESS CALLING ADDRESS RESPONDING ADDRESS RECEIPT CONFIRMATION SELECTION EXPEDITED DATA SELECTION QOS PARAMETER SET USER DATA	C
N-DATA	CONFIRMATION REQUEST USER DATA	U
N-DATA-ACKNOWLEDGE		U
N-EXPEDITED-DATA	USER DATA	U
N-RESET	ORIGINATOR REASON	C
N-DISCONNECT	ORIGINATOR RESPONDING ADDRESS REASON USER DATA	U/P

Figure 6.6 Summary of Network Layer primitives

NSDU. To take another example, a reset object is defined to be destructive of user data ahead of it in the queue: resetting of the network connection is modelled as the introduction of a reset object to the queue, with consequent loss of user data in the queue ahead of it.

Network services are provided by the exchange of four types of primitive between the Network and Transport Layers: request, indication, response and confirm primitives. An unconfirmed network service is provided by use of request and indication primitives only; a confirmed network service requires use of all four types of primitive. The primitives used to provide the individual network services are shown in Figure 6.6, together with their associated parameters and the type of service (U — unconfirmed, C — confirmed, P — provider-initiated).

The use of a network connection by transport entities has three distinct phases:

- network connection establishment phase
- data transfer phase
- network connection release phase

Network connection establishment is provided by the Network Connection Establishment service. An exchange of N-CONNECT primitives between network and transport entities takes place, together with a supporting exchange of NPDUs between corresponding network entities across the data link connection (see Figure 6.7). These exchanges allow the characteristics of the desired network connection to be determined, including the quality of service parameters. The parameters conveyed by N-CONNECT primitives have the following uses:

- called address — used by request and indication primitives to convey an address identifying the NSAP to which the network connection is to be made
- calling address — used by request and indication primitives to convey an address identifying the NSAP from which the network connection originated
- responding address — used by response and confirm primitives to convey an address identifying the NSAP to which the network connection has actually been made
- receipt confirmation selection — used by all N-CONNECT primitives to indicate whether the Receipt Confirmation service is available and, if so, whether it is going to be used by this network connection
- expedited data selection — used by all N-CONNECT primitives to indicate whether the Expedited Data Transfer service is available, and if so, whether it is going to be used by this network connection
- QOS-parameter set — used by all N-CONNECT primitives for the negotiation of the quality of service to be established for the network connection

- user data — used to transfer NSDUs between transport entities during network connection establishment

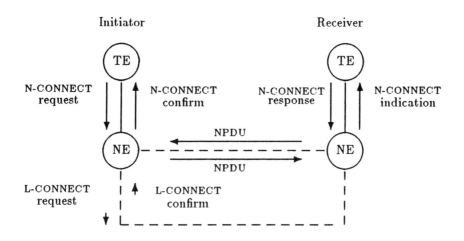

Figure 6.7 Network Connection Establishment service

The use of the QOS-parameter set parameter is a major feature of the Network Connection Establishment service. In order to provide an efficient negotiation of quality of service, each member of the QOS-parameter set has a number of subparameters, each of which may take a number of values, including the value 'unspecified'. Default values may also be defined. The network performance parameters negotiated by the QOS-parameter set are:

- throughput — specifies the rate of transfer of NSDUs with unconstrained flow control. It may be different for each direction of transfer
- transit delay — the elapsed time between an N-DATA request and the corresponding N-DATA indication in the Data Transfer service. This is the same for both directions of transfer

Other QOS-parameters are not negotiated, but are measurements of subnetwork performance, or characteristics of the network service. The negotiation of throughput and transit delay is based on the following four types of values:

- target — the value desired by the calling network service user
- lowest quality acceptable — the lowest value agreeable to the calling network service user
- available — the value which the network service is willing to provide
- selected — the value to which the called network service user agrees

Once negotiated, the quality of service is maintained for the duration of a network connection.

The *data transfer* phase includes the following services:

- Data Transfer service
- Receipt Confirmation service (optional)
- Expedited Data Transfer service (optional)
- Reset service (optional)

The Data Transfer service is provided by the N-DATA request and indication primitives and allows for the exchange of NSDUs between network service users. The only parameter, besides user data which contains the NSDU, is confirmation request. This parameter is used to request that the Receipt Confirmation service be invoked by the receiving network service user.

The Receipt Confirmation service allows a receiving network service user to acknowledge receipt of NSDUs. It is provided by the N-DATA-ACKNOWLEDGE primitives, which have no parameters. An N-DATA-ACKNOWLEDGE request is issued by the receiving network service user on receipt of each N-DATA indication primitive having the confirmation request parameter set.

The Expedited Data Transfer service is an unconfirmed service provided through the use of the N-EXPEDITED-DATA primitive, whose only parameter is expedited user data (ENSDU). The transfer of ENSDUs across the subnetwork is subject to different flow control and quality of service from that established on the network connection for the Data Transfer service. As described earlier,

ENSDUs may bypass NSDUs in the queues. However, it cannot be guaranteed that they will be able to bypass a blockage in normal data flow which occurs in a lower layer.

The Reset service uses the N-RESET primitives to provide a confirmed service. An N-RESET request may be issued by a network service user to resynchronize use of the network connection, in which case it has one parameter, reason, which takes the value 'user resynchronization'. An N-RESET indication which is issued without an associated request allows the network service provider to report congestion of the network connection, or loss of user data within the network service. It conveys two parameters: originator, which takes the value 'network service provider', and reason, which takes either the value 'congestion' or the value 'unspecified'. There are a number of possible sequences of exchanges in the provision of the Reset service, one of which is shown in Figure 6.8.

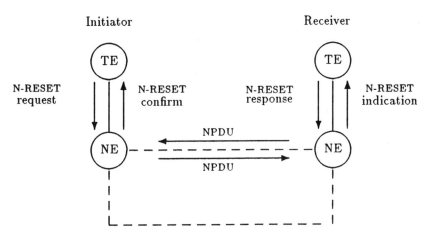

Figure 6.8 Reset service invoked by network service user

The use of the Reset service causes the Network Layer to discard all NSDUs, ENSDUs or confirmation of receipts associated with the network connection, and inform any user which did not invoke the service that reset has occurred. The N-RESET primitives placed in the queues act as markers in the flows of NSDUs and ENSDUs, at which the flows are synchronized by the network service provider.

Network connection release is provided by a single unconfirmed service, the Network Connection Release service, which makes use of the N-DISCONNECT primitives to release a network connection. Release may be initiated either by the network service users or by the network service provider. There are four possible connection release scenarios:

- an established network connection may be released by either network service user

- the network service provider may release an established network connection, indicating a failure in the connection

- the called network service user may reject the request for initial connection

- the network service provider may be unable to establish a network connection in response to a connection request

A request for connection release may be made at any time, regardless of the current state of the network, and cannot be rejected; consequently data still in transit may be lost.

The sequence in which primitives are transferred and the content of the parameter fields are dependent on the connection release scenario. The parameters are as follows:

- originator — source of the request for connection release, indicating network service user or provider

- reason — reason for the connection release

- user data — allowed only if the connection release has been initiated by a network service user

- responding address — the address of the NSAP from which the request for disconnection originated (used only when a network service user is rejecting a request for connection)

Figure 6.9 illustrates the transfer of primitives in normal connection release, where the release of a network connection is initiated by one of the connected network service users.

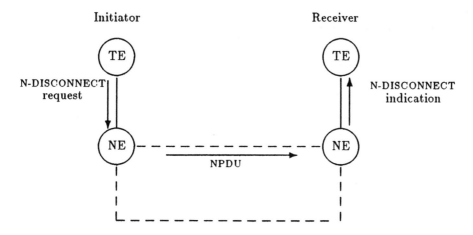

Figure 6.9 Network Connection Release service

In addition to the services described above, the Network Layer needs to provide conversion between the connection-oriented and connectionless modes of data transmission. In particular, it should provide the functions necessary to build a connection-oriented network service on a connectionless Data Link Layer.

The connectionless network service (CLNS) can be seen as a simplified version of the connection-oriented network service. Instead of NPDUs being transferred in two directions over a pre-established connection, data transfer in the CLNS is a series of single, self-contained events. Connection establishment and release are unnecessary, and data transfer can be modelled as a single, one-way queue between two network service users. The service is provided by N-UNITDATA request and indication primitives which contain the following parameters:

- destination address — address of destination transport entity

- source address — address of originating transport entity

- quality of service — as requested by originating transport entity

- user data — data for transfer between transport entities

Each NPDU in the CLNS thus contains all that is necessary for the routeing and transfer of data across real subnetworks, with a quality of service chosen by the originating transport entity. There is no provision for acknowledgement of receipt and the CLNS will not necessarily report cases of non-delivery. In addition, there is no guarantee that data units will be delivered in the same order as they were presented for delivery; it must be a function of higher layers to ensure that data units are processed by the receiving open system in the correct order.

6.3   Discussion of Technologies

Probably the best known protocol in use for the Network Layer is that specified by CCITT recommendation X.25. In fact, X.25 pre-dates the OSI model by a considerable time. It provides a specification for the lower three layers of the OSI model, but in this chapter we will only consider the packet level protocol which is the part of the X.25 recommendation that pertains to the OSI Network Layer. In this section the concepts of X.25 are related to the provision of an OSI connection-oriented network service. There are two main versions of X.25 which are currently implemented: the 1980 recommendation and the 1984 recommendation. For the purposes of this book, the 1984 recommendation will be described.

In the specification of the Data Link Layer given in Chapter 5, the provision for primary and secondary stations was discussed. In specifications of the Network Layer a similar provision may be made, which defines subsets of Network Layer functions and elements of protocol, allowing network entities to operate in different modes. The terms commonly used to indicate these different modes of network entity operation within real subnetworks are:

- data terminal equipment (DTE) — a real end system whose network entity has no routeing or relaying function

- data circuit-terminating equipment (DCE) — an intermediate system whose network entity has only a routeing and relaying function

The term 'DXE' is used where the context makes it unnecessary to distinguish between a DTE and a DCE.

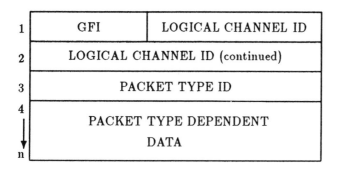

GFI (GENERAL FORMAT IDENTIFIER) — 4 bits

LOGICAL CHANNEL ID — a number indicating the logical
number of the connection, 12 bits

PACKET TYPE ID — a binary pattern identifying the
packet type, 8 bits

Figure 6.10 General X.25 packet format

The X.25 recommendation specifies the protocol for the exchange of data between a DTE and a DCE (that is, a packet-switched subnetwork) at the packet (or Network) level. Direct DTE to DTE communication is also specified. All data transfers consist of packets of information sent over a virtual circuit connection between X.25 packet layer users. It should be noted that a packet in X.25 terms is a unit of data with a predefined format which is sent and received at the packet level of X.25. This has no relationship to the term 'packet' used to mean a unit of data transmitted through a packet-switched network. X.25 packets all have the same general format, with an additional amount of data dependent on the type of packet. The general packet format is shown in Figure 6.10.

A set of packet types, each of which performs a particular function, is defined by X.25. A full list of the available packet types is shown in Figure 6.11. As can be seen from the figure, some of the packet types are known by different names depending on whether they are being sent by or received by the DTE. Regardless of the packet names, the packet type identifier is fixed for a single packet

DTE sends	DTE receives
CALL REQUEST	INCOMING CALL
CALL ACCEPTED	CALL CONNECTED
CLEAR REQUEST	CLEAR INDICATION
CLEAR CONFIRM	CLEAR CONFIRMATION
DATA	DATA
INTERRUPT	INTERRUPT
INTERRUPT CONFIRM	INTERRUPT CONFIRM
RECEIVE READY	RECEIVE READY
RECEIVE NOT READY	RECEIVE NOT READY
REJECT	REJECT
RESET REQUEST	RESET INDICATION
RESET CONFIRM	RESET CONFIRM
RESTART REQUEST	RESTART INDICATION
RESTART CONFIRM	RESTART CONFIRM
DIAGNOSTIC	DIAGNOSTIC
REGISTRATION REQUEST	REGISTRATION REQUEST
REGISTRATION CONFIRM	REGISTRATION CONFIRM

Figure 6.11 X.25 packet types

type.

The functions performed by each packet type are as follows:

- Call Request — requests the establishment of a switched virtual circuit (SVC) between two X.25 users

- Call Accepted — acknowledges and accepts the establishment of an SVC

- Clear Request — requests the release of an SVC which was established by a Call Request

- Clear Confirm — acknowledges and accepts the release of an SVC

- Data — transmits user data over a virtual circuit as governed by the flow control procedures

- Interrupt — transmits user data over a virtual circuit without regard to flow control procedures

- Interrupt Confirm — acknowledges the receipt of an Interrupt packet
- Receive Ready — indicates readiness to receive data packets starting from the packet number contained within the Receive Ready packet
- Receive Not Ready — indicates a temporary inability to receive Data packets
- Reject — requests a retransmission of an invalid Data packet
- Reset Request — resets a virtual circuit to an initialised state with the transmit and receive counters set to zero
- Reset Confirm — acknowledges and accepts the receipt of a Reset Request packet
- Restart Request — resets the whole DTE/DXE interface resulting in the clearance of all active virtual circuits across that interface
- Restart Confirm — acknowledges and accepts the receipt of a Restart Request packet
- Diagnostic — indicates error conditions to a DTE
- Registration Request — allows online registration for the use of optional user facilities
- Registration Confirm — confirms the registration for use of optional user facilities

Sequences of these packets are used to support communication between a DTE and the destination DXE. A simple dialogue could be:

- DTE sends a Call Request and receives a Call Connected
- Data packets are transmitted in either direction
- when the dialogue is complete, the DTE sends a Clear Request and receives a Clear Confirm indicating that the call has been cleared

Each Data packet has a sequence number which is allocated to it on either a modulo-8 or modulo-128 basis, and each packet must be acknowledged by the receiver.

The transmission of Data packets is limited by a 'sliding window' flow control mechanism. Each of the two communicating systems has a *window* of packets which it can transmit. The window is the number of packets which may be sent before an acknowledgement is required. Acknowledgements can either be 'piggy backed' on incoming Data packets, or can be explicit in incoming Receive Ready or Receive Not Ready packets. Either way, the receiver has control of when the sender may send packets. As X.25 operates in a full duplex manner, flow control and data transfer can take place in both directions at the same time.

Reference 6.2 describes how recommendation X.25 may be used to provide the OSI connection-oriented network service (CONS). Not all of the packet types of X.25 are required to support the CONS — specifically Clear Confirm, Reset Confirm, Restart Request, Restart Confirm, Diagnostic and the two registration packets are not required. However, although they are not required by the OSI Network Layer standard, some of the packet types are essential to the operation of X.25, and as such must be available. The following facilities, which are optional for X.25, are mandatory for the CONS:

- fast select
- fast select acceptance
- throughput class negotiation
- transit delay selection and indication
- called address extension
- calling address extension
- end to end transmit delay
- expedited data negotiation
- minimum throughput class negotiation

Figure 6.12 shows a mapping between Network Layer primitives and the X.25 packet types required to implement them.

The relationship between the OSI CONS and X.25 is not completely straightforward, and is further complicated by the existence of the two (1980 and 1984) versions of X.25. X.25 (1984) supports a network service by means of the *subnetwork access control protocol*

OSI CONS	X.25
N-CONNECT request	CALL REQUEST
N-CONNECT indication	INCOMING CALL
N-CONNECT response	CALL ACCEPTED
N-CONNECT confirm	CALL CONNECTED
N-DATA request	DATA
N-DATA indication	DATA
N-DISCONNECT request	CLEAR REQUEST
N-DISCONNECT indication	CLEAR INDICATION
	or RESTART INDICATION
	or CLEAR REQUEST
N-EXPEDITED-DATA request	INTERRUPT
N-EXPEDITED-DATA indication	INTERRUPT
N-RESET request	RESET REQUEST
N-RESET indication	RESET INDICATION
	or RESET REQUEST
N-RESET response	none
N-RESET confirm	none

Figure 6.12 Primitive to packet mapping

(SNACP), which allows communication between open systems using X.25 (1984). X.25 (1980) does not provide the same degree of functionality as the later version of X.25, and in order to support a network service, the *subnetwork dependent convergence protocol* (SNDCP) is required in addition to the SNACP. Communication is made possible between open systems using different versions of X.25 by the use of multiple protocols (see Figure 6.3).

6.4   References

6.1 *Open Systems Interconnection: connection-mode network service definition* (DD 119), British Standards Institution, 1985. (This Draft for Development is the equivalent of ISO/DIS 8348.)

6.2 *Open Systems Interconnection: use of X.25 to provide the connection-oriented network service* (DD 122), British Standards Institution, 1985. (This Draft for Development is the equivalent of ISO/DP 8878.)

6.3 *Open Systems Interconnection: X.25 packet level protocol for data terminal equipment* (DD 117), British Standards Institution, 1985. (This Draft for Development is the equivalent of ISO/DIS 8208.)

6.4 *Open Systems Interconnection: protocol for providing the connectionless-mode network service* (DD 118), British Standards Institution, 1985. (This Draft for Development is the equivalent of ISO/DIS 8473 and ISO/DIS 8348 DAD 1.)

6.5 *Open Systems Interconnection: internal organization of the network layer* (DD 135), British Standards Institution, 1985. (This Draft for Development is the equivalent of ISO/DP 8648.)

6.6 *Open Systems Interconnection: network layer addressing* (DD 134), British Standards Institution, 1985. (This Draft for Development is the equivalent of ISO/DIS 8348 DAD 2.)

6.7 *Open Systems Interconnection: naming and addressing* (DD 149), British Standards Institution, 1986. (This Draft for Development is the equivalent of ISO 7498/PDAD 3.)

7 Transport Layer – Layer 4

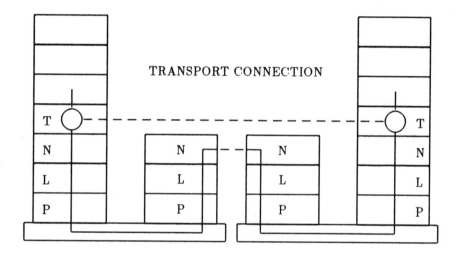

TRANSPORT CONNECTION

The Transport Layer is the highest layer in the OSI model which is directly involved with data communications. The network service provides routeing and relaying across real subnetworks, possibly involving the use of intermediate open systems; the transport service, in contrast, is concerned only with communication between *end* open systems and has no interest in the route actually taken by data travelling between those end systems. Its responsibility is to provide session entities with a reliable, cost-effective means of transferring data, protecting them from needing to know anything about the underlying real data communications system. The Transport Layer thus links the layers below, which are responsible for transmitting data across real subnetworks, with the layers above, which are responsible for maintaining an orderly dialogue between application processes in end open systems.

Continuing the telephone analogy from previous chapters, the transport service is equivalent to the total service provided by the telephone system. Lifting the receiver and dialling a destination telephone number is the equivalent of requesting a transport connection, and when the destination handset is lifted, the transport connection is established. In order to make this connection, the telephone user need only know the destination telephone number, the equivalent of a transport address. The telephone user has no need to know how the call is routed, how many exchanges it goes through or what sort of transmission medium is used. Once the telephone connection has been established, any number of telephone users may use it without having to redial or disconnect. When the telephone users have finished with the connection they hang up, the equivalent of a transport disconnection. Again, there is no need for them to know about the links between intermediate exchanges which are cleared as they hang up.

The Transport Layer is responsible for the overall selection and control of all available network services in an open system. It is the layer which balances the requirements of the whole population of transport service users over the whole range of possible network connections.

7.1   Requirements for Layer 4

The Transport Layer is required to provide the following services:

- transport connection establishment — to allow the quality of service parameters for the connection to be determined

- data transfer — to provide reliable and transparent transfer of transport service data units (TSDUs) between session entities in end open systems

- transport connection release — to provide the means by which either corresponding session entity may release the transport connection

In order to support these services, the Transport Layer also performs the following functions:

- mapping of the transport address onto the network address

- multiplexing of transport connections onto network connections

- monitoring of the quality of service

- end-to-end sequence and flow control

- error detection and recovery

- segmenting, blocking and concatenation

- supervisory functions

- expedited data transfer

The Transport Layer is also responsible for *optimisation* of network service usage. It controls and allocates all available network services, so as to provide the quality of service required by each of the transport service users (that is, session entities) as cheaply as possible. The overall capacity and quality of the available network service are also taken into account.

The Transport Layer must be capable of making use of different types and qualities of network service. The amount of work required of the transport service varies depending on the quality of the available underlying network connections. For poor quality network connections, the Transport Layer requires additional error handling facilities to be able to ensure the quality of the transport connection. To formalise the levels of service required of the Transport Layer, network connections are divided into three types depending on their reliability. Five different transport protocol classes are also defined, each of which is designed to be used in a particular way over a particular type of network connection. A more detailed description of these facilities is provided in the following section.

The transport services are provided through use of transport protocols. These protocols may only be used between end open systems, and they are therefore described as having *end-to-end significance*. Transport protocols are implemented using transport protocol data units (TPDUs) which are exchanged between connected transport entities.

7.2   Specification of Layer 4

The extent of the functions performed in the Transport Layer is dependent on both the quality of service required by the requesting session entity and the quality of connection provided by the network service. In many cases, the available network connections may not be adequate to provide the required quality of service: the transport service must then provide functions to add value to the network service so as to provide an acceptable service to its users.

The transport service provided to a session entity is divided into three phases:

- transport connection establishment
- data transfer
- transport connection release

The *transport connection establishment* phase consists of selecting the network connection most appropriate to meet the requirements of the requesting session entity, and deciding on which set of transport functions is required to support the connection. When these selections have been made and agreed on by the transport entities at both ends of the connection, the connection is established.

The session entity may request a certain *quality of service* from the transport service at connection time. The quality of service of a transport connection is a description of the operating characteristics of that connection and is specified by means of the following parameters:

- transport connection establishment delay
- transport connection establishment failure probability
- throughput
- transit delay
- residual error rate
- transfer failure probability
- transport connection release delay
- transport connection release failure probability

- transport connection protection

- transport connection priority

- resilience of the transport connection

The requested quality of service may be reduced during negotiation either by the transport service provider or by the called transport service user. When the quality of service negotiation has been completed, both ends of the transport connection have the same view of the quality of service available over that connection.

As has been stated previously, the amount of work required of the transport service depends on the services provided by the Network Layer. To assist in identifying the functions required from the transport service, network connections have been classified into three network connection *types* on the basis of their error characteristics. The error characteristics used are the residual error rate (that is, the ratio of incorrect TSDUs transferred to the total number of TSDUs transferred) and the rate of signalling failures (that is, the number of network disconnect or reset signals received). The network connection types available are as follows:

- Type A — a connection where both the residual error rate and the rate of signalling failures are acceptable

- Type B — a connection where the residual error rate is acceptable, but the rate of signalling failures is unacceptable

- Type C — a connection where the residual error rate is unacceptable

It should be noted that these network types are not absolute. They are defined in terms of acceptability to transport service users and what is acceptable to one user may not be acceptable to another. In order to allocate connection requests to the appropriate network connection and to provide the correct transport functions, each transport entity must be aware of the quality of service provided by each network connection.

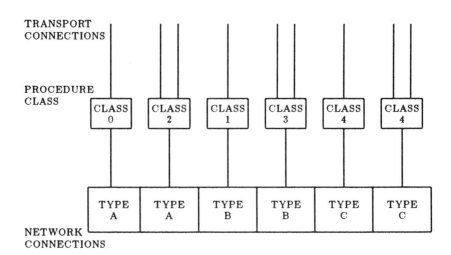

Figure 7.1 Procedure classes and network connection types

During the *data transfer* phase, TSDUs are exchanged between session entities over the transport connection. Two types of data transfer are available: normal data transfer and expedited data transfer.

When the data transfer is complete, a *transport connection release* is performed. The release of a transport connection may be requested at any time by either of the connected transport entities or by the transport service provider. When initiated by the transport service provider during the connection establishment phase, the release indicates that the transport service provider is unable to provide the services required by the transport service user. A provider-initiated release during the data transfer phase indicates that the service being used has failed to meet its requirements. The release of a transport connection may free the Network Layer resources which had been selected to support it.

Functions performed by the transport service are grouped into *classes* of procedure. The relationship between classes of procedure and network connection types is shown in Figure 7.1. There are five classes of procedure numbered from zero to four as follows:

- Class 0, the simple class
- Class 1, the basic error recovery class
- Class 2, the multiplexing class
- Class 3, the error recovery and multiplexing class
- Class 4, the error detection and recovery class

The procedure class to be used and the options within that procedure class are negotiated when a transport connection is established. The procedure classes will now be described in more detail.

Class 0, the simple class, provides the minimum functionality as it is designed for use on a network connection where the basic quality of service is acceptable to the requesting session entity (that is, a Type A connection). Class 0 provides the following functions:

- assignment to a network connection
- connection establishment with limited parameters
- limited Data TPDU size
- implicit connection release

The duration of a connection under Class 0 is directly related to the duration of the underlying network connection. There is no facility for releasing a transport connection without releasing the network connection and *vice versa*.

Class 1, the basic error recovery class, provides recovery from errors signalled by the Network Layer (through the provider-initiated network connection release or reset services). This class is designed for use on a network connection where the residual error rate is acceptable to the requesting session entity, but the rate of signalling failures is unacceptable (that is, a Type B connection). The error recovery procedures are provided to counteract the shortfall in the network quality of service. The functions provided by Class 1 are the same as those provided by Class 0 with the addition of:

- recovery from failure signalled by the network service
- expedited data transfer
- explicit connection release

Transport connections under Class 1 must be explicitly released and so are not tied to the availability of the underlying network connection. The transport connection will be maintained throughout network connection failure and recovery. A transport connection release will not necessarily result in the release of a network connection; in fact, the network connection may be re-used by subsequent transport connections.

Class 2, the multiplexing class, provides the same functionality as Class 0, but with additional support for multiplexing more than one transport connection over a single network connection. This class is provided for use over a Type A connection. The following facilities are provided in addition to those provided by Class 0:

- multiplexing
- flow control (using the credit mechanism described later in this chapter)
- exchange of user data during connection establishment
- expedited data transfer
- explicit connection release

The use of an explicit transport connection release mechanism and multiplexing allows individual transport connections to be released with no effect on the underlying network connection. However, if the network connection is lost, all transport connections using that network connection are lost.

Class 3, the error recovery and multiplexing class, provides the equivalent functionality of Class 2 with the addition of error recovery for errors signalled by the Network Layer. This class is used to support multiplexing of transport connections over a Type B connection.

Class 4, the error detection and recovery class, provides support of single or multiplexed connections over a Type C network connection (that is, a connection with an unacceptable residual error rate). This class provides the functionality of Class 3 with additional facilities to provide transparent recovery from errors in the receipt of TPDUs. These errors include lost, duplicated, out of sequence or corrupted TPDUs. The main additional facilities provided by Class 4 are:

- timeout mechanisms
- checksums
- use of multiple network connections for a single transport connection (connection splitting)

As the network connection quality in Class 4 is by definition unsatisfactory, the procedure for establishing a transport connection consists of a three-way exchange rather than the normal two-way confirmed exchange. The timeout mechanisms are used to detect the loss of TPDUs in transit, and the checksum mechanism is used to detect data corruption within TPDUs.

Flow control over a transport connection can be divided into two separate types: Network Layer flow control and peer-to-peer flow control. The transmission of data over a transport connection is always limited by the flow control of the network connection which supports it. The Network Layer exerts a 'back-pressure' mechanism on the requesting transport entities; that is, the Network Layer will only accept data for onward transmission if the destination network entity is prepared to accept it. The Network Layer flow control mechanisms are described in more detail in Chapter 6.

Peer-to-peer flow control within the Transport Layer may be provided in addition to Network Layer flow control. The transport connection may be modelled in the same way as the network connection: that is, as a pair of shared queues between connected transport service access points (TSAPs) (see Figure 7.2). A transport service user can add objects to its outgoing queue and remove objects from

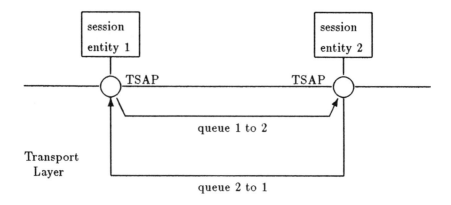

Figure 7.2 Transport connection modelled as a pair of queues

its incoming queue. However, the receiving session entity has control over the addition of objects to the queue by the sending session entity.

The ability of a receiving session entity to control the size of its incoming queue is dependent on an exchange of TPDUs containing flow control parameters. Transport Layer flow control uses a credit mechanism rather than the sliding window mechanism used in X.25 implementations of the Network Layer. Each Data TPDU has a serial number associated with it, and each of the communicating transport entities has a transmission window of serial numbers it is allowed to send. The transmission window is delimited by lower and upper window edges: the lower window edge is the current setting; the upper window edge is the sum of the lower window edge and the current credit value. The lower window edge is set and the upper window edge is derived during connection establishment. Both edges are changed by the receipt of an Acknowledgement TPDU, which contains a new setting for the lower window edge and a new credit value. The new upper window edge is then the new lower window edge plus the new credit value.

PRIMITIVE	PARAMETERS	TYPE	TPDUs
T-CONNECT	CALLED ADDRESS CALLING ADDRESS EXPEDITED DATA OPTION QUALITY OF SERVICE USER DATA (32 octets) RESPONDING ADDRESS	C	CR CC
T-DATA	USER DATA (unlimited)	U	DT AK RJ
T-EXPEDITED-DATA	USER DATA (16 octets)	U	ED EA
T-DISCONNECT	DISCONNECT REASON USER DATA (64 octets)	U/P	DR DC

Figure 7.3 Summary of Transport Layer primitives

By using this mechanism, the receiving transport entity limits the number of Data TPDUs which the sending transport entity can send, and consequently controls the number of TSDUs placed in the queue by the sending session entity. It should be noted that this method of flow control requires explicit acknowledgement which cannot be 'piggy backed' onto another Data TPDU.

Each of the classes of procedure provides some form of flow control. Classes 0 and 1 only use the flow control provided by the underlying Network Layer, while Classes 3 and 4 provide the explicit peer-to-peer flow control described above. Class 2 may choose whether to use peer-to-peer flow control on a connection by connection basis.

The transport service is provided to cooperating session entities through the exchange of Transport Layer primitives. These primitives and their associated parameters are shown in Figure 7.3, together with the TPDUs which are exchanged between transport entities in order to provide the transport service. The type of service provided is also indicated (U — unconfirmed, C — confirmed, P — provider-initiated).

For the Physical, Data Link and Network Layers, there is no

specific OSI definition of the layer protocols. Layer services and functions are defined by OSI standards, but protocols are defined only in terms of specific implementation standards such as HDLC and X.25. For the Transport Layer, and each of the layers above, OSI defines a layer protocol, which details the sequence and contents of protocol data units exchanged during the provision of the layer services.

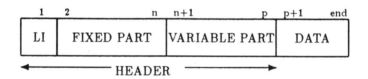

LI = LENGTH OF HEADER EXCLUDING LI

Figure 7.4 General TPDU format

The overall structure of TPDUs is shown in Figure 7.4. There are ten types of TPDU, each having its own specific format, and in some cases a particular TPDU has both a normal and an extended format. The detailed formats for TPDU types are listed in Figure 7.5, and their contents are shown as follows:

- LI — length indicator, the length of the TPDU header excluding the LI field

- octet 2 — a binary code indicating the type of TPDU. In the Connection Request (CR-TPDU), Connection Confirm (CC-TPDU), normal Reject (RJ-TPDU) and normal Acknowledgement (AK-TPDU) TPDUs, the least significant four bits contain the flow control credit value

- DST-REF — a reference identifying the transport connection at the remote transport entity. It has a value of zero in a CR-TPDU

- SRC-REF — a reference identifying the transport connection at the transport entity initiating the TPDU

NORMAL

	1	2	3	4	5 6	7	8 p	p+1 end
CR	LI	1110 CDT	0	0	SRC-REF	OPT-CLS	VARIABLE	USER DATA

	1	2	3 4	5 6	7	8 p	p+1 end
CC	LI	1101 CDT	DST-REF	SRC-REF	OPT-CLS	VARIABLE	USER DATA

	1	2	3 4	5 6	7	8 p	p+1 end
DR	LI	1000 0000	DST-REF	SRC-REF	REASON	VARIABLE	USER DATA

	1	2	3 4	5 6	7 end
DC	LI	1100 0000	DST-REF	SRC-REF	VARIABLE

	1	2	3	4 end	
DT	LI	1111 0000	TDPU-NR EOT	USER DATA	(Classes 0 and 1)

	1	2	3 4	5	6 p	p+1 end
DT *	LI	1111 0000	DST-REF	TPDU-NR EOT	VARIABLE	USER DATA

	1	2	3 4	5	6 p	p+1 end
ED	LI	0001 0000	DST-REF	EDTPDU-NR EOT	VARIABLE	USER DATA

	1	2	3 4	5	6 end
AK	LI	0110 CDT	DST-REF	YR-TU-NR	VARIABLE

	1	2	3 4	5	6 end
EA	LI	0010 0000	DST-REF	YR-TU-NR	VARIABLE

	1	2	3 4	5
RJ	LI	0101 CDT	DST-REF	YR-TU-NR

	1	2	3 4	5	6 end
ER	LI	0111 0000	DST-REF	CAUSE	VARIABLE

EXTENDED — selected during connection establishment

	1	2	3 4	5 6 7 8	9 p	p+1 end
DT *	LI	1111 0000	DST-REF	TPDU-NR EOT	VARIABLE	USER DATA

	1	2	3 4	5 6 7 8	9 p	p+1 end
ED *	LI	0001 0000	DST-REF	EDTPDU-NR EOT	VARIABLE	USER DATA

	1	2	3 4	5 6 7 8	9 10	11 end
AK *	LI	0110 0000	DST-REF	YR-TU-NR	CDT	VARIABLE

	1	2	3 4	5 6 7 8	9 end
EA *	LI	0010 0000	DST-REF	YR-TU-NR	VARIABLE

	1	2	3 4	5 6 7 8	9 10	
RJ	LI	0101 0000	DST-REF	YR-TU-NR	CDT	(Class 3)

* Classes 2, 3 and 4

Figure 7.5 TPDU formats

- OPT-CLS — bits 8 to 5 identify the protocol class to be used for a connection, bits 4 to 1 identify the options to be used. Possible options are the use of extended formats in Classes 2, 3 and 4 and the use of explicit flow control in Class 2

- VARIABLE — the variable part of the TPDU containing optional parameters

- USER DATA — the area containing the user data to be transmitted. In the CC-TPDU and the CR-TPDU the maximum size is 32 octets, in the Disconnect Request TPDU (DR-TPDU) 64 octets and in the Expedited Data TPDU (ED-TPDU) 16 octets. In the Data TPDU (DT-TPDU) the maximum size is the length of the TPDU (as negotiated at transport connection) minus the length of the other fields in the TPDU

- REASON — an indication of the reason for requesting a disconnection

- TPDU-NR — the sequence number of this TPDU

- EOT — an indicator that the TPDU is the last in a set of linked TPDUs (that is, the end of a TSDU)

- EDTPDU-NR — identification number of an Expedited Data TPDU

- YR-TU-NR — a number indicating the next expected Data TPDU sequence number

- CAUSE — a code indicating the reason for a TPDU rejection

- CDT — the flow control credit value

The sequence of TPDUs exchanged to provide the transport services involves different procedures depending on the protocol class selected for the requested connection. The following paragraphs show how the transport services are provided for each class of procedure.

The Connection Establishment service is provided by the T-CONNECT primitive sequence and the exchange of CR-TPDUs and CC-TPDUs. There are two different types of transport connection dialogue, one for use under protocol Classes 0 to 3 and one for use under protocol Class 4. All classes other than Class 4 use the following two-way connection dialogue (see Figure 7.6):

- the initiating session entity issues a T-CONNECT request primitive to a transport entity
- the transport entity selects an appropriate network connection and formats and sends a CR-TPDU over that connection. (The network connection may have to be activated first)
- the destination transport entity receives the CR-TPDU, formats a T-CONNECT indication and passes it to the destination session entity
- the destination session entity issues a T-CONNECT response to the destination transport entity
- the destination transport entity formats and sends a CC-TPDU to confirm the connection, possibly with some changes to the parameters
- the initiating transport entity receives the CC-TPDU, formats a T-CONNECT confirm and passes it to the initiating session entity
- the transport connection is now established

A transport connection under Class 4 is established in a similar way, but using a three-way dialogue. On receipt of the CC-TPDU, the initiating transport entity responds by transmitting an AK-TPDU to acknowledge the connection. The reason for the addition of this extra step is to cater for problems caused by the issue of duplicate connection requests due to delays in the transmission of the original connection request.

The variable part of the CR-TPDU can contain a selection of the following parameters:

- calling TSAP ID — the identifier of the calling TSAP
- called TSAP ID — the identifier of the destination (or called) TSAP
- maximum TPDU size —the proposed maximum length of a TPDU to be enforced during the transport connection

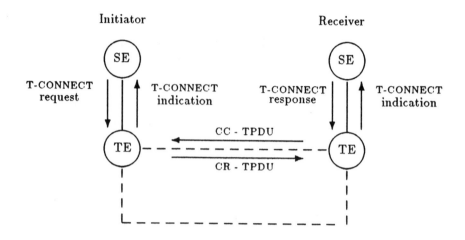

Figure 7.6 Two-way connection establishment

- version number — the version of the transport protocol standard to be used for this connection

- security parameters — user defined security parameters

- checksum — the calculated checksum used for Class 4 only

- additional option selection — a bit pattern indicating which additional options are required

- alternative protocol class — an indication of an acceptable alternative protocol class if the preferred class is unacceptable

- acknowledge time — an indication of the maximum elapsed time between receipt of a TPDU by the local transport entity and the transmission of an acknowledgement

- throughput — an indication of the throughput required for the requested connection

- residual error rate — an indication of the required residual error rate

- priority — an assignment of priority to the requested connection, zero being the highest priority

- transit delay — an indication of the maximum acceptable transit delay for the connection

- reassignment time — an indication of the time to wait before attempting to assign a transport connection to a new network connection after a network connection failure

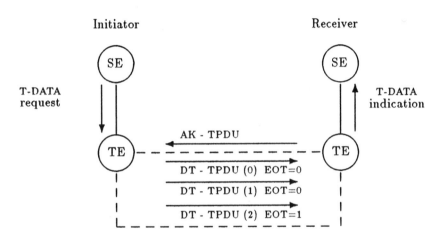

Figure 7.7 Data Transfer service

The Data Transfer service provided by the Transport Layer is an unconfirmed, one-way service, but the underlying transport protocol interactions are two-way and may include flow control and rejection of invalid TPDUs. The following is an example of one-way data transfer with explicit flow control (see Figure 7.7):

- the initiating session entity issues a T-DATA request containing a user data parameter which requires (for the purpose of this example) three TPDUs to be sent

- the transport entity sends three Data TPDUs, the last of which indicates that it is the end of the TSDU

- the receiving transport entity receives the DT-TPDUs and

sends an AK-TPDU to acknowledge and to open up the transmission window

- the receiving transport entity formats and sends a T-DATA indication primitive to the receiving session entity

Another possibility for data transfer is the service provided by T-EXPEDITED-DATA primitives, which allows for a very limited amount of user data (16 bytes) to be transmitted in such a way that it may be inserted between DT-TPDUs which are being transmitted consecutively. For example, in Figure 7.7 an Expedited Data TPDU could be interposed between DT-TPDUs (1) and (2) without causing any disruption.

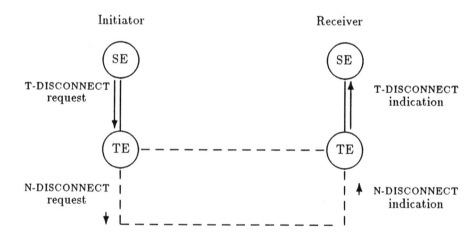

Figure 7.8 Implicit disconnection

The Connection Release service may be provided in two ways, implicitly and explicitly. The implicit form as used by protocol Class 0 releases both the transport and the network connections with no exchange of TPDUs between transport entities. The steps performed are as follows (see Figure 7.8):

- the initiating session entity sends a T-DISCONNECT request to the transport entity

- the transport entity issues an N-DISCONNECT request
- the receiving transport entity receives an N-DISCONNECT indication and formats and sends a T-DISCONNECT indication to the receiving session entity
- the transport connection is now released

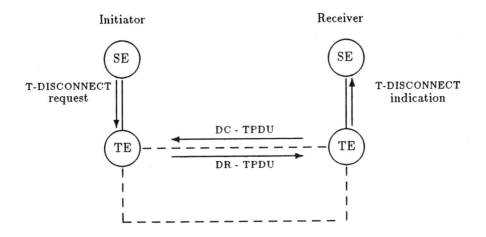

Figure 7.9 Explicit disconnection

The explicit variant of the transport connection release involves the exchange of disconnection requests and may leave the network connection available for subsequent transport connections. The steps to be performed for an explicit disconnection are as follows (see Figure 7.9):

- the initiating session entity issues a T-DISCONNECT indication
- the transport entity formats and sends a Disconnect Request TPDU (DR-TPDU)
- the receiving transport entity receives the DR-TPDU, formats a T-DISCONNECT indication and passes it to the receiving session entity

- the receiving transport entity formats and sends a Disconnect Confirm TPDU (DC-TPDU) to acknowledge the release

- when the initiating transport entity receives the DC-TPDU, the transport connection is released

This discussion of the Transport Layer has dealt exclusively with the connection-oriented transport service. OSI, however, includes a connectionless transport service provided by T-UNITDATA primitives. Each TSDU is transmitted in a single, independent access to the transport service, with no connection being established or released. As with the connectionless network service (see Chapter 6), the connectionless transport service can be modelled as a single, one-way queue, into which only data unit objects may be placed by the initiating transport service user.

7.3   Discussion of Technologies

The definition of the OSI Transport Layer (and of the layers above it) has taken place ahead of the development of technologies implementing the layer standards. This is in contrast with Layers 1 to 3, where the OSI layer standards have been written sufficiently broadly to include a number of technologies which existed before OSI. In Chapters 4 to 6, therefore, OSI-compliant technologies (such as the packet level of X.25 in the Network Layer) have been dealt with at some length. This section, however, can only be a brief survey of the application areas which currently make use of the layer services.

Implementations of the OSI Transport Layer are now widely available from many major computer manufacturers. In some cases Transport Layer services are provided as part of functional standards to meet specific requirements. For example, the Manufacturing Automation Protocol (MAP) and the Technical Office Protocols (TOP) both require the use of Transport Layer Class 4. The OSI Transport Layer is also required for Layer 4 of the CCITT X.400 message handling system recommendations.

7.4   References

7.1   *Open Systems Interconnection: transport service definition* (DD 115), British Standards Institution, 1985. (This Draft for Development is the equivalent of ISO/DIS 8072 and DAD 1.)

7.2   *Open Systems Interconnection: transport proctocol specification* (DD 116), British Standards Institution, 1985. (This Draft for Development is the equivalent of ISO/DIS 8073 and DAD 1.)

7.3   *Open Systems Interconnection: proctocol to provide the connectionless-mode transport service utilizing either the connectionless-mode or the connection-oriented network service* (DD 137), British Standards Institution, 1985. (This Draft for Development is the equivalent of ISO/DB 8602.)

8 Session Layer – Layer 5

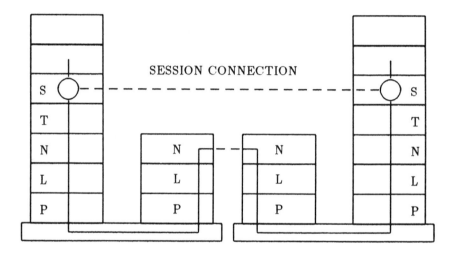

For most people, the mechanisms of communication are unimportant. If you want to tell a friend something, the structure of your conversation will be the same regardless of whether you are face to face in the same room, or thousands of miles apart at opposite ends of a telephone connection. For your conversation to take place, all you really need to know is that some means exists for your partner to hear what you say and *vice versa*.

Any conversation between two people can be broken down into three phases:

- gaining your partner's attention and agreement to talk
- exchanging information
- ending the conversation

Before any conversation can take place, both participants must agree to take part — the equivalent of the first phase. Having agreed to holding the conversation, information is exchanged as one party talks and the other listens — the second phase. When there is no more to be said, the conversation is ended and both participants go their separate ways — the final phase.

In the context of the OSI reference model and computer to computer communications, the Session Layer provides session service users (that is, presentation entities) with the means to carry on their communication. The Session Layer enables the presentation entities to establish a connection, exchange information in an orderly way and finally it enables the connection to be terminated — a sequence of functions broadly corresponding to the three phases of a telephone conversation outlined above.

The Session Layer forms a bridge between those layers which are wholly concerned with providing a data transportation mechanism (Layers 1 to 4) and those layers which are more closely involved with applications and their data (Layers 6 and 7). It makes use of the data transfer services provided by Layers 1 to 4 to supply a transparent communications capability to the layers above it. The functions of the Session Layer, as described in section 8.2, combine to provide a connection-oriented session service for presentation entities, where a connection (or association) must be established between applications if they are to communicate with each other. When the association has been made, information may be transferred until the connection is released.

The analogy of a conversation taking place across a telephone connection, as introduced earlier, is useful in describing some of the facilities provided by the Session Layer. Establishing a session connection is the equivalent of ensuring that your destination party is available at the other end of a telephone connection and that he is willing to talk to you. (Note that establishment of the telephone connection would not be necessary if the telephone link were already open.)

Having established the connection, the two communicating parties can exchange information, usually in two-way alternate mode. (A two-way simultaneous exchange of information is a bit tricky in a human conversation, for obvious reasons!) The conversation can continue until it reaches some agreed end, at which point one of the parties initiates a connection release by saying 'Goodbye' or something similar. The other party then has the option of accepting the release by also saying 'Goodbye', or of indicating that he wishes to continue the conversation — 'Hold on, what about.....'

At any time during the conversation it is possible for information to be lost, or for either of the communicating parties to miss a sentence and get confused. Asking someone to repeat something, or to start again from a particular point in a conversation is similar to the resynchronizing facility of the Session Layer. The analogy diverges a little here as the synchronization points are only implied in a telephone conversation, whereas the session service establishes specific synchronization points.

In the case of a more serious disruption to the telephone call, one of the parties may be asked to repeat a whole conversation, which may even have taken place over more than one call. This is the equivalent of restarting an activity within the session service.

8.1 Requirements for Layer 5

The main requirement of the Session Layer is to provide for the organization and synchronization of a dialogue between two session service users, and to allow those users to manage their data exchange.

This requirement is fulfilled by the provision of the following services to the Presentation Layer:

- session connection establishment — to allow two presentation entities to establish a session connection between them and to agree on the rules to be enforced for that connection

- normal data exchange — to allow for the transfer of data between connected presentation entities

- session connection release — to allow the release of a connection between two presentation entities either in an orderly way with no loss of data, or as an immediate release with the loss of any outstanding data

- quarantine service — to allow a sending presentation entity to identify a number of session service data units (SSDUs) which will not be released to the destination presentation entity until specifically released by the sending presentation entity. (Note that although this service is specified in the OSI model, a mechanism to support it has not been developed to the stage where it can be included in the current Session Layer standard)

- expedited data exchange — to allow SSDUs of limited size to be transferred as expedited data which bypasses the normal data flow and which may overtake messages which have already been sent

- interaction management — to allow control of which communication partner may initiate certain functions

- service connection synchronization — to allow two communicating presentation entities to synchronize their communication by the insertion of known synchronization points

- exception reporting — to allow for the reporting of errors to associated presentation entities

The Session Layer provides a large range of facilities, many of which may not be required for a particular implementation. To save on time and implementation costs, implementations are allowed by OSI to contain a limited subset of the facilities available. This subset need only be enough to support the requirements of the upper layers: unwanted functions may be left out provided the rules for defining subsets are observed. In any case, the functions to be used during a particular session connection will be negotiated at connection time. The least facility-rich of the two systems must always win in such negotiations: it is possible not to use facilities which are available, but it is impossible to use facilities which are not available.

This method of grouping facilities into Session Layer subsets allows an implementation to identify which parts of the session service it claims to have implemented. The particular functions included in an implementation will depend on the requirements of the upper layers. A number of subsets are defined by the standards, but implementors may also define their own subsets of functions. A fuller discussion of this topic can be found in section 8.2.

8.2   Specification of Layer 5

In order to fulfil the requirements identified in section 8.1, the Session Layer provides a set of session services to presentation entities. Before looking at the detailed functions of session services, some basic concepts will be explained.

Synchronization — one of the services mentioned in section 8.1 was session synchronization. Two communicating presentation entities may wish to insert synchronization points in their dialogue, a practice similar to the insertion of restart points in a long batch job. It allows the two communicating presentation entities to ensure that there are fixed points in their dialogue which both recognise. These points can then be used for resynchronization of the session and recovery to a mutually agreed point.

The session service provides for the insertion of two types of synchronization point:

- major synchronization point
- minor synchronization point

The major synchronization point divides a data exchange into dialogue units. A dialogue unit starts and ends with a major synchronization point and is treated as if it were unrelated to data exchanges before and after it. A dialogue unit may itself be divided by the insertion of minor synchronization points. The session service provides a mechanism to allow communicating presentation entities to synchronize. However this does not imply any action from the Session Layer in maintaining checkpoints or retaining data for retransmission, which must be done by the application externally to the OSI environment.

An example of the use of synchronization points could be the transfer of a data file. The whole file transfer may be one dialogue unit, and minor synchronization points may be inserted every hundred records or so to allow for a restart in the event of a failure.

Synchronization is supported by the following session services:

- Minor Synchronization Point service — allows for the insertion of minor synchronization points in the exchange of data

- Major Synchronization Point service — allows for the data exchange to be divided into dialogue units by the insertion of major synchronization points

- Resynchronize service — allows for the data exchange to be resynchronized at a previously specified major or minor synchronization point

Activities — presentation entities may wish to identify data exchanges which are logically related over and above the specification of synchronization points. An example of this could be the transfer of a collection of files making up a database. Each of the files could be one dialogue unit as discussed earlier, and the whole database transfer could be an activity. Activities may be started, ended, suspended, recovered and discarded. By use of suspend and resume services, an activity may be split over more than one session connection.

The following session services support the use of activities:

- Activity Start service — allows a new activity to be started

- Activity Interrupt service — allows the current activity to be ended, but implies that it may be restarted later

- Activity Resume service — allows for the continuation of a previously interrupted activity

- Activity Discard service — allows the current activity to be ended and indicates that the previous content of the activity should be discarded

- Activity End service — allows the current activity to be ended; this also has the effect of setting a major synchronization point

Tokens — it is desirable that some of the session services should only be available to one or other of the communicating presentation entities at a time. To enforce this, a mechanism is required to indicate who has the right to carry out a restricted function: the Session Layer makes use of tokens to control access to restricted functions, particular tokens being associated with selected session services. A token may, however, be unavailable, in which case use of the restricted service depends on the type of token. In some cases, neither of the communicating parties can use the service; in other cases, both parties can use it. Where the token is available, it is allocated to one of the communicating presentation entities, which then controls the restricted function. Tokens can be passed between communicating presentation entities in order to exchange control.

There are four tokens which may be used:

- the data token — used to designate who is allowed to send data when two-way alternate working (half duplex) is in use

- the release token — used to designate who is allowed to initiate a connection release

- the synchronize minor token — used to allow the token holder to insert minor synchronization points in the message dialogue

- the major/activity token — used to allow the holder to insert major synchronization points in the message dialogue, and also to initiate activities. If activities are in use, the services which support them are only available to the holder of this token

The concept of token usage is demonstrated in radio telephone communication, where by convention the current speaker says 'Over' to indicate that the other party may now speak. By saying 'Over', the direction of traffic is reversed — the equivalent in the Session Layer of passing the data token from one presentation entity to another.

The following services allow session service users to control the allocation of tokens:

- Give Token service — allows a session service user to pass specified tokens to the other user. This may be used in response to a please token

- Please Token service — allows a session service to request the transfer of specified tokens from the other user

- Give Control service — allows a session service user to pass all available tokens to the other user

1	2	3	n n+1	end

SI	LI	PARAMETERS	USER DATA

SI = SPDU IDENTIFIER

LI = LENGTH OF PARAMETER FIELD

Figure 8.1 General SPDU format

SPDUs — data is transferred between session entities by means of session protocol data units (SPDUs). Each SPDU contains an identifier to indicate its type, a variable length parameter field with a preceding length indicator and some optional user data. The general format of an SPDU is shown in Figure 8.1, but actual SPDU formats vary depending on parameter usage. If there are no parameters, the parameter field is omitted and the length field (LI) is set to zero. For a single parameter, as shown in Figure 8.2, the parameter field contains the parameter identifier (PI), the length of the parameter value field (LI) and the parameter value field. The length of the parameter field as a whole is held in the LI field preceding the parameter information. As a further complication, parameters can be grouped into parameter groups as in Figure 8.3. Each parameter group has a parameter group identifier (PGI) and a length indicator containing the total length of all parameter information within that parameter group. The parameter field of the SPDU can contain several parameter groups.

In the discussion of synchronization, activities, token usage and session protocol data units, a number of the functions of the Session Layer have already been identified and described. These functions support the Session Layer as it fulfils its primary functions, namely session connection, data transfer, exception reporting and connection release. These will now be covered in turn, together with their associated services.

PI	LI	PV

PI = PARAMETER IDENTIFIER

LI = LENGTH OF PV FIELD

PV = PARAMETER VALUE

Figure 8.2 Parameter field with single parameter

PGI	LI	PARAM 1	PARAM 2

PGI = PARAMETER GROUP IDENTIFIER

LI = LENGTH OF PARAM 1 AND PARAM 2

PARAM 1 and PARAM 2 are parameter fields in the same format
as the single parameter shown in Figure 8.2

Figure 8.3 Parameter field with parameter group

The establishment of a *session connection* is provided by a single
service:

- Session Connection service — allows for the establishment of
  a session connection and the negotiation of the rules to apply
  for the duration of that connection

The *data transfer* services provide for the exchange of data in
different circumstances. There are four data transfer services:

- Normal Data Transfer service — allows for the transfer of
  normal data over a session connection. Data transfer may be

full or half duplex, but if half duplex is used, the data token must be used to indicate who is allowed to send data

- Expedited Data Transfer service — allows for the transfer of expedited data over a session connection making use of the expedited data transport service. Expedited data may overtake normal data during transmission. The data token is not required for expedited data transfer

- Typed Data Transfer service — allows for the transfer of a limited amount of data when the data token is not held by the initiator (that is, against the current flow of data)

- Capability Data Exchange service — allows for the confirmed transfer of a limited amount of data when activity services are available but there is no activity currently in progress. This service is required because normal data transfer is not allowed if the use of activities has been negotiated but the session connection is currently between activities. If the data token is available, capability data can only be sent by the owner of the data token

The *exception reporting* services allow for the exchange of error information between the session service user and the session entity. There are two exception reporting services:

- Provider-Initiated Exception Reporting service — allows a session service user to be informed of any errors or unexpected situations detected by the session service provider

- User-Initiated Exception Reporting service — allows a session service user to inform the session service provider of error situations

The *session termination* services provide a means of terminating the current session connection either by a controlled release or by an abort. There are three session termination services:

- Orderly Release service — allows the orderly release of the current session connection without the loss of data. If the release token is available, the release can only be initiated by the token release holder

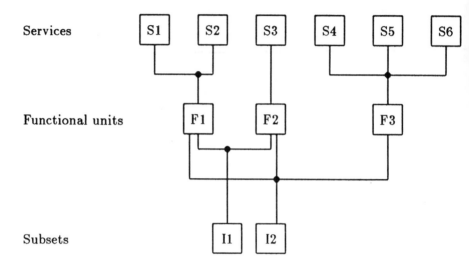

Figure 8.4 Relationship between services, functional units and subsets

- User-Initiated Abort service — allows a session service user to abort the current session connection with the possible loss of data
- Provider-Initiated Abort service — allows a session service provider to indicate to a session service user that its current connection has been aborted with a possible loss of data

It has been found convenient to group session services into *functional units*, logical groupings of functions which can be used to provide a particular type of service. Functional units provide a means for referring to groups of services, during, for example, negotiation of the services to be used for the duration of a session connection. Particular implementations of the Session Layer may be defined in terms of the functional units they include.

Subsets are groupings of functional units which may be implemented to provide a subset of the session service. All subsets must contain the Kernel functional unit, along with a number of other functional units. The relationship between services, functional units and subsets is shown in Figure 8.4, where services S1 and S2 form functional unit F1, and functional units F1 and F2 form subset I1. The groupings of session services into functional units are shown in Figure 8.5.

Three subsets are defined by the standard:

- Basic Combined subset (BCS) which comprises

  - Kernel
  - Half Duplex
  - Duplex

- Basic Synchronized subset (BSS) which comprises

  - Kernel
  - Negotiated Release
  - Half Duplex
  - Duplex
  - Typed Data
  - Minor Synchronize
  - Major Synchronize
  - Resynchronize

- Basic Activity subset (BAS) which comprises

  - Kernel
  - Half Duplex
  - Typed Data
  - Capability Data Exchange
  - Minor Synchronize
  - Exceptions
  - Activity Management

Other subsets may be defined as required by implementors, but they must comply with the following basic rules:

FUNCTIONAL UNIT	SERVICE(S)
Kernel	Session Connection
	Normal Data Transfer
	Orderly Release
	User-Initiated Abort
	Provider-Initiated Abort
Negotiated Release	Orderly Release
	Give Tokens
	Please Tokens
Half Duplex	Give Tokens
	Please Tokens
Duplex	no additional service
Expedited Data	Expedited Data Transfer
Typed Data	Typed Data Transfer
Capability Data Exchange	Capability Data Exchange
Major Synchronize	Major Synchronization Point
	Give Tokens
	Please Tokens
Minor Synchronize	Minor Synchronization Point
	Give Tokens
	Please Tokens
Resynchronize	Resynchronize
Exceptions	Provider-Initiated Exception Reporting
	User-Initiated Exception Reporting
Activity Management	Activity Start
	Activity Resume
	Activity Interrupt
	Activity Discard
	Activity End
	Give Tokens
	Please Tokens
	Give Control

Figure 8.5 Session Layer functional units and related services

- The Kernel functional unit must always be included as it contains the minimum services to maintain a session service
- The Capability Data Exchange functional unit can only be included in subsets which contain the Activity Management functional unit
- If the Exceptions functional unit is included in a subset, the Half Duplex functional unit must also be included

Having described the services provided by the Session Layer, some of the detailed processing carried out on behalf of a session service user can now be considered. As stated previously, there are three distinct phases of Session Layer operation:

- session connection establishment phase
- data transfer phase
- session connection release phase

The *session connection establishment* phase consists of the processing required to establish a session connection between two consenting presentation entities. The following parameters are passed as part of the S-CONNECT primitive to allow the communicating session entities to agree on the rules for the connection:

- session connection identifier — the means by which session service users will identify the connection
- called and calling session service access point (SSAP) addresses
- result — indicates the success or failure of the connection request
- quality of service — indicates the requirements of the connection in terms of throughput, transit delay and other associated areas
- session requirements — a list of functional units to be available for the connection
- initial synchronization point number

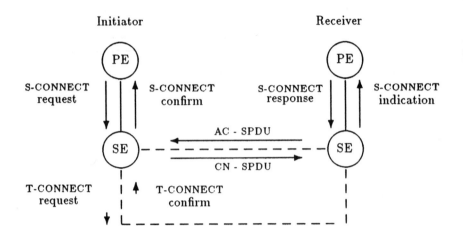

Figure 8.6 Establishing a session connection

- initial assignment of tokens — indicates the initial assignment for each of the available tokens

- user data — up to 512 octets of user information

Session Connection is a confirmed service which consists of the following steps, as shown in Figure 8.6:

- the initiating presentation entity issues an S-CONNECT request primitive to a session entity

- if there is no existing transport connection to the destination system, a T-CONNECT request is sent to the associated transport service access point (TSAP). On receipt of a T-CONNECT confirm, the transport connection is available

- a Connection Request SPDU (CN-SPDU) is formatted and sent to the destination session entity (via the transport service using a T-DATA request)

- the called session entity receives the CN-SPDU (via a T-DATA indication) and issues an S-CONNECT indication to the destination presentation entity

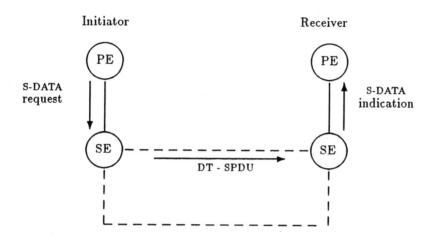

Figure 8.7 Normal Data Transfer service

- the destination presentation entity formats an S-CONNECT response indicating its willingness to accept the connection, and indicating its agreement or otherwise with the negotiated parameters

- the called session entity uses the S-CONNECT response to format an Accept Connect SPDU (AC-SPDU) and sends it to the calling session entity

- the calling SSAP receives the AC-SPDU and issues an S-CONNECT confirm to the initiating presentation entity

The *data transfer* phase consists of the processing required to transfer data between connected presentation entities. This phase also includes the services for dialogue management and synchronization.

The Normal Data Transfer service allows the requesting presentation entity to send data to its communication partner. The only parameter passed with this primitive is user data which consists of an unlimited number of octets of data. Normal Data Transfer is an unconfirmed service consisting of the following steps (see Figure 8.7):

- the initiating presentation entity issues an S-DATA request to the session entity
- a Normal Data SPDU (DT-SPDU) is formatted and sent to the receiving Session Entity
- the receiving session entity formats an S-DATA indication and passes it on to the destination presentation entity

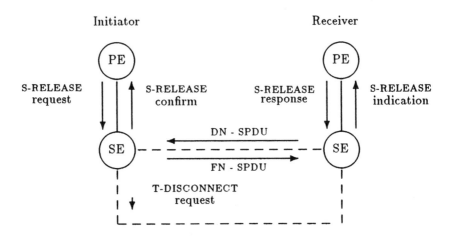

Figure 8.8 Orderly Release service

The *session connection release* phase consists of the processing required to release a connection between two presentation entities. The connection release may be orderly, in which case both connected presentation entities agree to release, or it may be an abort, in which case either the presentation entity or the session service provider decides to abort a connection with the possible loss of data.

The Orderly Release service may be initiated by either of the connection partners unless the Negotiated Release functional unit has been selected. In this case only the current holder of the release token may initiate the release. The orderly release of a session connection consists of the following steps (see Figure 8.8):

- the initiating presentation entity issues an S-RELEASE request

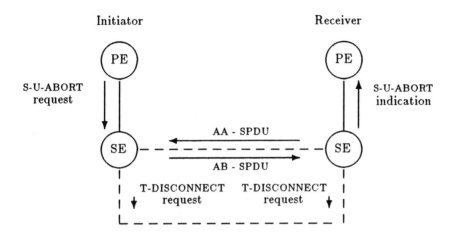

Figure 8.9 User-Initiated Abort service

- a Finish SPDU (FN-SPDU) is formatted and sent to the receiving session entity
- the receiving session entity issues an S-RELEASE indication to the receiving presentation entity
- the receiving presentation entity issues an S-RELEASE response indicating that it accepts the release request
- the receiving session entity formats a Disconnect SPDU (DN-SPDU) and sends it to the initiating session entity
- the initiating session entity receives the DN-SPDU and issues an S-RELEASE confirm to the initiating presentation entity
- if re-use of the transport connection is not required, a T-DISCONNECT is issued to clear the transport connection

The session connection is now terminated.

The User-Initiated Abort service may be requested at any time during a connection by either of the connected presentation entities. The abort request will use the expedited data transport service (if available) and so may overtake data transmitted on the normal data transport service. Although this could result in the loss of messages, an abort usually indicates a serious problem — the issuing user would probably be unable to handle pending messages in an abort situation. The user abort of a connection consists of the following steps (see Figure 8.9):

- the initiating presentation entity issues an S-U-ABORT request

- an Abort SPDU (AB-SPDU) is formatted and sent to the receiving session entity (using the expedited data transport service if available)

- the receiving session entity issues an S-U-ABORT indication to the receiving presentation entity

- if the AB-SPDU as received indicated that the transport connection should be retained, or if the expedited data transport service is not available, the receiving session entity sends an Abort Accept SPDU (AA-SPDU) to the initiating session entity

- if the transport connection is no longer required, the receiving session entity issues a T-DISCONNECT primitive

- the initiating session entity may receive either an AA-SPDU or a T-DISCONNECT indication — both indicate completion of the abort. If an AA-SPDU is received, the initiating session entity may issue a T-DISCONNECT request to complete the termination

A provider abort may occur at any time during a session connection. It may be triggered by several different events: for example, the loss of a transport connection or a protocol error. The Provider-Initiated Abort service may consist of the following steps (see Figure 8.10):

- the initiating session entity detects an error situation

- the initiating session entity issues an S-P-ABORT indication to the presentation entity

- the initiating session entity formats an AB-SPDU and sends it to the receiving session entity

- the receiving session entity issues an S-P-ABORT indication to the receiving presentation entity

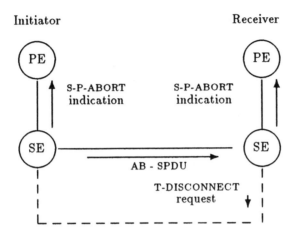

Figure 8.10 Provider-Initiated Abort service

- depending on the reason for the abort, the receiving session
  entity may issue a T-DISCONNECT request

The provider abort may be initiated as a consequence of problems
in any of the layers below the connected session entities. As may
be imagined, there are many possible reasons for an abort: the case
outlined above is only one possible scenario and must serve as an
example for the others too numerous to describe here.

All the Session Layer primitives are shown in tabular form in
Figure 8.11. For each primitive, the primitive name, the associated
parameters, the type of service (U — unconfirmed, C — confirmed,
P — provider-initiated) and the associated SPDUs are given.
Primitives associated with connection establishment, data transfer
and connection release have already been described at length. Most
of the other Session Layer primitives operate in a standard manner,
and only two exceptions need be explained in any further detail.

The first of the exceptions is the Give Control service, which is
unusual for an unconfirmed service in having two SPDUs associated
with it. Give Control allows for the transfer of all available tokens

PRIMITIVE	PARAMETERS	TYPE	SPDUs
S-CONNECT	SESSION CONNECT ID	C	CN
	CALLING SSAP		AC
	CALLED SSAP		RF
	RESULT		
	QUALITY OF SERVICE		
	SESSION REQS		
	INITIAL SYNC NUMBER		
	INITIAL TOKENS		
	USER DATA (512 octets)		
S-DATA	USER DATA (unlimited)	U	DT
S-EXPEDITED-DATA	USER DATA (14 octets)	U	EX
S-TYPED-DATA	USER DATA (unlimited)	U	TD
S-CAPABILITY-DATA	USER DATA (512 octets)	C	CD
			CDA
S-TOKEN-PLEASE	TOKENS		
	USER DATA (512 octets)	U	PT
S-TOKEN-GIVE	TOKENS	U	GT
S-CONTROL-GIVE	NONE	U	GTC
			GTA
S-SYNC-MINOR	TYPE	C	MIP
	SYNC NUMBER		MSA
	USER DATA (512 octets)		
S-SYNC-MAJOR	SYNC NUMBER	C	MAP
	USER DATA (512 octets)		MAA
S-RESYNCHRONIZE	RESYNC TYPE	C	RS
	SYNC NUMBER		RA
	RESYNC TOKENS		
	USER DATA (512 octets)		
S-P-EXCEPTION-REPORT	REASON	P	ER
S-U-EXCEPTION-REPORT	REASON	U	ED
	USER DATA (512 octets)		
S-ACTIVITY-START	ACTIVITY ID	U	AS
	USER DATA (512 octets)		
S-ACTIVITY-INTERRUPT	REASON	C	AI
			AIA
S-ACTIVITY-RESUME	ACTIVITY ID	U	AR
	OLD ACTIVITY ID		
	SYNC NUMBER		
	OLD SESSION CONNECT ID		
	USER DATA (512 octets)		
S-ACTIVITY-DISCARD	REASON	C	AD
			ADA
S-ACTIVITY-END	SYNC NUMBER	C	AE
	USER DATA (512 octets)		AEA
S-RELEASE	RESULT	C	DN
	USER DATA (512 octets)		FN
S-U-ABORT	USER DATA (9 octets)	U	AB
			AA
S-P-ABORT	REASON	P	AB

Figure 8.11 Summary of Session Layer primitives

and the two SPDUs are necessary to allow the session entities at each end of the connection to change to the current state. This service may only be used when the Activity Management functional unit has been selected and there is no activity currently in progress. The following steps are required (see Figure 8.12):

- the initiating presentation entity issues an S-CONTROL-GIVE request to the session entity via the SSAP

- a Give Tokens Confirm SPDU (GTC-SPDU) is formatted and sent to the receiving session entity

- the receiving session entity formats an S-CONTROL-GIVE indication and passes it to the destination presentation entity

- a Give Tokens Acknowledge SPDU (GTA-SPDU) is then formatted and returned to the initiating session entity

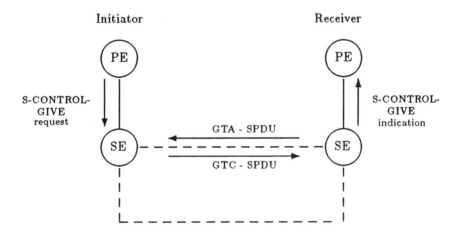

Figure 8.12 Give Control service

The second exception is the Prepare SPDU (PR-SPDU), which is associated with the data transfer phase. The PR-SPDU may be issued using the expedited data transport service to give the remote session entity advance warning of the arrival of a particular SPDU on the normal data transport service. There are three possible types of Prepare SPDU:

- Prepare for Major Synchronize Acknowledge SPDU

- Prepare for Resynchronize SPDU

- Prepare for Resynchronize Acknowledge SPDU

8.3 Discussion of Technologies

The development of the Session Layer standard has been heavily influenced by the existence of other external standards, a particular example being the CCITT T.62 recommendations on control procedures for Teletex and Group 4 Facsimile services. These recommendations have had considerable influence on the session protocol data unit format in the area of parameters and parameter groups. Some parameter identifiers and parameter group identifiers are not specifically defined in the standard, but are reserved for use by T.62.

Various subsets of the session services are required for different application services: for example, implementors of MAP (Manufacturing Automation Protocol) and TOP (Technical Office Protocols) will require the Basic Combined subset, but implementors of FTAM (File Transfer, Access and Management) will also require the Minor Synchronization and Resynchronization functional units.

The Session Layer standard is not static. Further developments are occurring which may have an impact on future issues of the Session Layer standard (Reference 8.1 and Reference 8.2). Particular areas of development are as follows:

- Quarantine service — although this service is mentioned in the OSI basic reference model standard (see Reference 3.1), it is not currently supported by the Session Layer standard

- Connectionless Transfer service — this service is being developed at the lower layers. The Session Layer should pass requests for this service to the Transport Layer with no changes other than the addition of protocol control information

- two-way synchronization — the mechanism provided by the standard only allows for synchronization in one direction and is two-way alternate in nature. Work has been carried out on the provision of synchronization in both directions of a two-way simultaneous flow. This work has reached the Draft Addendum (DAD) stage

- security — work is continuing on security aspects of the OSI model as a whole, but the Session Layer has been identified as the only layer where no security considerations apply

8.4   References

8.1 *Open Systems Interconnection: basic connection-oriented session service definition* (DD 111), British Standards Institution, 1985. (This Draft for Development is the equivalent of ISO/DIS 8326 revised.)

8.2 *Open Systems Interconnection: basic connection-oriented session protocol specification* (DD 112), British Standards Institution, 1985. (This Draft for Development is the equivalent of ISO/DIS 8327 revised.)

9 Presentation Layer – Layer 6

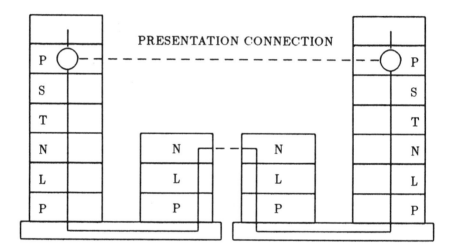

The layers described in the preceding chapters provide the services necessary for one system to transfer data to another. What these layers cannot guarantee is that the receiver understands the sender's data. Telephones may allow you to speak to your Chinese counterpart in Peking, but unless you can agree to conduct your communication in a commonly understood language, your telephone conversation will be merely a meaningless exchange of sounds.

It is no surprise, therefore, that one layer of the OSI model is concerned with the form in which data is presented to communication partners, which in OSI are entities in the Application Layer. It is the function of the Presentation Layer to format data correctly for its users, the application entities which correspond to the speakers in the telephone conversation analogy given above. In our example, assuming that you and your Chinese counterpart speak no common language, it would be necessary to have the services of a translator (or translators) before beginning the conversation. The equivalent within OSI would occur when an application running on an IBM machine and using EBCDIC needed to communicate with an application using ASCII (on a DEC computer, for example). In this case, the applications would be supported by a pair of connected presentation entities, which would agree on conversion between EBCDIC and ASCII and *vice versa*. If this conversion did not take place, *data* could be transferred between applications, but the destination application entity would not receive meaningful *information*. The Presentation Layer provides applications with a representation of the transferred data which they can understand. In OSI, the way in which data is represented is known as *context*, a term whose precise meaning is explained in section 9.2.

It may well be that you wish your conversation to be private from listening ears or as short as possible (to reduce your telephone bill!), in which case you may decide to use some sort of 'scrambling' device or request your translator not to echo any long pauses you may have had in your dictation. Data communication equivalents of this are encryption and compression, which can also be handled by the Presentation Layer, although encryption can occur in other layers. Data is encrypted or coded by the sender and decoded by the receiver using known 'keys'; an example of a compression technique would be the replacement of repeated characters by a single character and a count.

9.1 Requirements for Layer 6

As described in the introduction to this chapter, the function of the Presentation Layer within the OSI model is to ensure the meaning of data transmitted between open systems is preserved. Simply expressed, this means that even if the data encodings (the syntaxes) as seen by the sender and receiver are different, the meaning of the data (the semantics) must be equivalent. The basic requirement for an implementation of the Presentation Layer, therefore, is that it must provide the following facilities:

- presentation connection establishment
- data transfer with information preservation

- presentation connection release

The connection establishment facility should allow application entities to define the characteristics of the presentation connection. These characteristics are concerned with which elements of the presentation service are required and an initial agreement on how communicated information can be represented.

Data transfer should, as a minimum, provide a means by which the information content of transmitted data can be presented to the recipient in an understandable form. If the corresponding session services are available (as described in Chapter 8), then the following additional elements can be provided:

- typed data transfer — used when the initiator does not own the data token and allows transfer of data against the current flow

- expedited data transfer — used to give a particular presentation service data unit (PSDU) an element of priority, so that it is delivered before all succeeding PSDUs and possibly before preceding PSDUs

- capability data exchange — used to transmit information outside an activity

The connection release facility should allow an agreed and orderly termination of the connection to occur without loss of data. In abnormal circumstances, it may be necessary to terminate the connection with a consequent loss of data: this should also be allowed by the connection release facility.

Other facilities which may optionally be provided by the Presentation Layer are:

- context management — allows a presentation service user to alter the data representation 'rules' of a connection

- context resynchronization — allows those rules in use at a particular time to be stored as a synchronization point so that they can be restored at some later stage of the connection, perhaps to recover from errors

Any implementation of the Presentation Layer must also embody the following:

- session service mapping
- extensibility

The services provided by the Presentation Layer must be compatible with the services offered by the Session Layer: the subset of services provided by the Session Layer must map onto at least one subset of the presentation services capable of supporting a presentation connection. The implementation must also allow for extensibility so as to be upwardly compatible with future enhancements to the standard. In this context, primitives containing unrecognised parameters should be accepted and the extra items ignored; where parameters have an associated maximum length, values in excess of that length should be accepted with the extra portion ignored.

9.2   Specification of Layer 6

As in the preceding chapters, before considering the detailed specification of the Presentation Layer, it is important to clarify some fundamental concepts.

Abstract syntaxes — presentation service users must adhere to some sort of convention of data representation for the information passed between them and the Presentation Layer. If this were not the case, an application could not guarantee that its data was being presented to its communication partner in an understandable form. The convention adhered to is known as an 'abstract syntax', a formal definition of data types and permissible values. An abstract syntax is best defined using a concise notational form.

The OSI standard abstract syntax notation is known as *Abstract Syntax Notation One* (ASN.1). The term ASN.1 is often used to refer to the formal description of data and also (incorrectly) to the rules for encoding the described data at bit level. The OSI standard encoding method is known as the *Basic Encoding Rules* (BER) and it is used to generate unambiguous representations of the data described using ASN.1. Within ASN.1 a formal syntax is used to define all possible data types, by tagging the data types with two attributes, *class* and *number*.

Four classes of data type are defined:

- universal — data types defined by the OSI standard
- private — data types defined for a particular implementation of OSI
- application — data types defined by a specific application within a particular implementation of OSI
- context specific — data types defined for use by a specific context

Each item within each class is given a unique number, so that each data type recognised by an OSI implementation is uniquely identified by a combination of class and number.

Data definitions in ASN.1 are similar to data definitions provided by programming languages such as PASCAL or ADA. Each item of data is assigned a name and a type, and defined items can be used to build up more complex data structures. Examples of definitions of items using a universal data type are:

- Requestcode   ::=   Integer
- Requestdata   ::=   IA5String

In these examples, Requestcode is an integer and Requestdata is a string of ASCII characters.

These two simple data structures may be combined to form a more complex structure as follows:

    Request   ::=   [APPLICATION 0] SEQUENCE
                    {Requestcode,
                    Requestdata}

Request is defined here as an application data type, number 0, which consists of a sequence of Requestcode followed by Requestdata. A request with a code of 1 and data of 'FRED' would be encoded as:

{Requestcode 1
Requestdata "FRED"}

BER encodes each data item such that it consists of the following:

- identifier octets — used to hold the ASN.1 tag
- length octets — used to indicate the length of the data in octets
- contents octets — used to hold the data

For example, the BER encoding of the simple request defined above would be:

Identifier   Length   Contents
H60   H09
(Request)

       Identifier   Length   Contents
       H02   H01   1
       (Integer)

       Identifier   Length   Contents
       H16   H04   "FRED"
       (IA5String)

(H = Hexadecimal)

Transfer syntax — the way in which the presentation service represents information in transit between presentation entities is known as the *presentation connection transfer syntax*. It is the role of the presentation service to transform the ASN.1 data contained in presentation service data units (PSDUs) received from a sending application entity into a previously agreed transfer syntax. This data is then transformed from the transfer syntax into the appropriate local syntax for delivery to the receiving application entity. It is here that such techniques as compression and encryption can be introduced.

Presentation context — whilst the presentation service is not responsible for the specification of abstract syntaxes used by application entities, it is responsible for the selection of appropriate transfer syntaxes used between presentation entities. The mapping of a transfer syntax with a particular abstract syntax is known as a *presentation context*. A presentation connection may allow several contexts to be used, constituting the *defined context set*.

Having completed our consideration of the fundamental Presentation Layer concepts, we shall define in turn each of the services the layer provides to its users — that is, application entities.

Presentation connection establishment involves the establishment of a presentation connection and is provided by a single service:

- Presentation Connection service — allows for the establishment of a presentation connection and its initial characteristics

The *information transfer* services provide for the exchange of information (including any necessary transformation) in four modes:

- Normal Data Transfer service — allows for the transfer of data over a presentation connection using a defined context
- Typed Data Transfer service — allows for the transfer of data over a presentation connection using a defined context when the data token is not held by the initiator
- Expedited Data Transfer service — allows for the transfer of data using the default context at a priority above that of other data transfers
- Capability Data Exchange service — allows for the transfer of data using a defined context outside an activity

Context alteration provides for the management of the defined context set by means of a single service:

- Alter Context service — allows for the negotiation of changes to the defined context set following connection establishment

The *connection termination* services provide the means to end the current connection either in a controlled manner or in an abort situation:

- Connection Release service — allows for a presentation service user to perform an orderly presentation connection termination without loss of data
- User Abort service — allows for a service user to abort a presentation connection with risk of loss of data
- Provider Abort service — allows a presentation entity to inform the user that the presentation connection has been lost, with possible loss of data

The following presentation services provide direct access to services provided by the Session Layer:

- Token Management service — allows access to the token control services of the Session Layer
- Synchronization service — allows access to the synchronization point services of the Session Layer
- Activity Management service — allows access to the activity control services of the Session Layer

For the same reasons which applied to services in the Session Layer, the Presentation Layer services are grouped together in functional units, of which there are three:

- Kernel — consisting of the connection establishment, information transfer and connection termination services
- Context Management — consisting of the context alteration and resynchronization services
- Context Restoration — providing access to the Activity Management, Major Synchronize, Minor Synchronize and Resynchronization functional units in the Session Layer

Implementations of the Presentation Layer must always include the Kernel functional unit. The Context Management functional unit may be selected with the Kernel, but the Context Restoration functional unit can only be selected in conjunction with both the other functional units.

The processing carried out by the presentation service on behalf of an application entity can be divided into three distinct phases:

- presentation connection establishment phase
- information transfer phase
- presentation connection release phase

The *presentation connection establishment* phase consists of the processing required to establish a presentation connection between two consenting application entities. The following parameters are passed as part of the P-CONNECT primitives transferred between the application and presentation entities to negotiate the characteristics of the connection:

- called and calling presentation service access point (PSAP) addresses
- responding PSAP address — used to establish the connection in the event of a failure
- multiple defined contexts — used to indicate if more than one defined context is required
- presentation context definition and result lists — used to indicate proposed initial defined context set members and the acceptability to the receiving system
- default context name and result — used to propose a default context and its acceptability to the receiving system
- quality of service — used to pass to the session service the connection requirements in terms of throughput and transit delay
- presentation requirements — used to indicate which presentation functional units are required by the connection
- session requirements — used to indicate which session functional units are required by the connection
- initial synchronization point number — used to access the session service parameter

- initial assignment of tokens — used to access the session service parameter
- session connection identifier — used to access the session service parameter
- user data — used to pass data (expressed in a defined context) between presentation service users
- result — used to indicate the outcome of the connection request

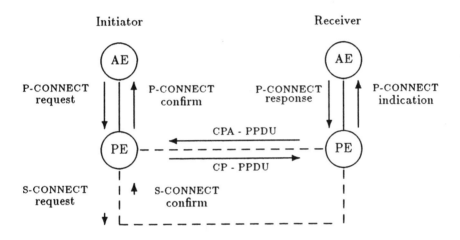

Figure 9.1 Establishing a presentation connection

Presentation Connection is a confirmed service which consists of the following steps (see Figure 9.1):

- the initiating application entity issues a P-CONNECT request primitive to a presentation entity
- the calling presentation entity formats and sends a Connection Presentation PPDU (CP-PPDU) to the called presentation entity (via the session service using an S-CONNECT request primitive)
- the called presentation entity receives the CP-PPDU (via an S-CONNECT indication) and issues a P-CONNECT indication to the receiving application entity

- the receiving application entity formats a P-CONNECT response indicating its willingness to accept the connection and agreement or otherwise with the negotiable parameters

- the called presentation entity uses the P-CONNECT response to format a Connect Presentation Accept PPDU (CPA-PPDU) and sends it to the calling presentation entity

- the calling presentation entity receives the CPA-PPDU and issues a P-CONNECT confirm to the initiating application entity

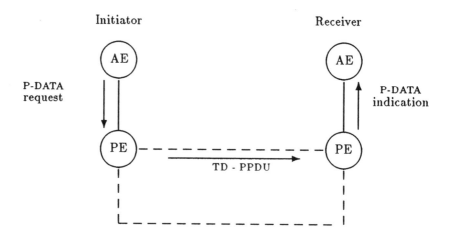

Figure 9.2 Normal Data Transfer service

The *information transfer* phase contains all the processing required to support the transfer of information between application entities. It includes not only the information transfer services themselves but also the Alter Context service and those of the session services which are accessible. Normal Data Transfer is the most important of the information transfer services available. The only parameter passed between the application and presentation entities during normal data transfer is the user data expressed using a defined context. Normal Data Transfer is an unconfirmed service consisting of the following steps (see Figure 9.2):

- the initiating application entity issues a P-DATA request primitive to its PSAP

- the calling presentation entity formats and sends a Presentation Data PPDU (TD-PPDU) to the called presentation entity (via the session service using an S-DATA request)

- the called presentation entity receives the TD-PPDU and issues a P-DATA indication to the receiving application entity

An important element of the information transfer phase is context management, specifically the Alter Context service. The defined context set of a presentation connection can be modified by negotiation between the communicating presentation entities. The basis and result of the modification are passed between the application and presentation entities using the following parameters contained within P-ALTER-CONTEXT primitives:

- presentation context definition and result lists — used to propose contexts for addition to the defined context set and to indicate the result of the proposals

- presentation context deletion and result lists — used to propose contexts for deletion from the defined context set and to indicate the result of the proposals

- user data — used to contain data to be passed between application entities using one of the defined contexts

Alter Context is a confirmed service which is only available if the Context Management functional unit has been selected. It consists of the following steps (see Figure 9.3):

- the initiating application entity issues a P-ALTER-CONTEXT request primitive to its PSAP

- the calling presentation entity formats and sends an Alter Context PPDU (AC-PPDU) to the called presentation entity (via the session service using an S-TYPED-DATA request)

- the called presentation entity receives the AC-PPDU and issues a P-ALTER-CONTEXT indication to the receiving application entity

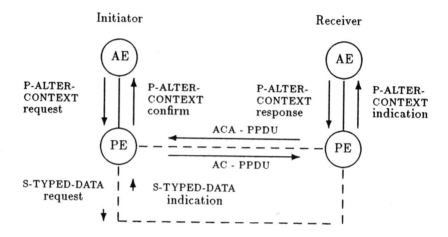

Figure 9.3 Alter Context service

- the receiving application entity issues a P-ALTER-CONTEXT response indicating its willingness to accept the alteration to the previously defined context set to the called presentation entity

- the called presentation entity formats and sends an Alter Context Acknowledge PPDU (ACA-PPDU) to the calling presentation entity

- the calling presentation entity receives the ACA-PPDU and issues a P-ALTER-CONTEXT confirm to the initiating application entity

The *presentation connection release* phase contains all the processing required to terminate presentation connections. As has been mentioned there are three ways in which a presentation connection can be terminated and it is worth describing each one individually.

Using the Connection Release service is the most common method of achieving connection termination. This service is performed using P-RELEASE primitives which contain the following parameters:

- user data — used to pass information between the communicating application entities, in one of the defined contexts
- result — used to indicate the result of the connection termination request

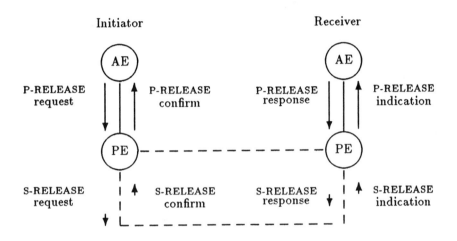

Figure 9.4 Connection Release service

Connection Release is a confirmed service and consists of the following steps (see Figure 9.4):

- the initiating application entity issues a P-RELEASE request primitive to its PSAP
- the calling presentation entity does not format any specific PPDU, but directly maps the P-RELEASE primitive onto an S-RELEASE primitive for the session service, which passes it to the called presentation entity as an S-RELEASE indication
- the called presentation entity issues a P-RELEASE indication to the receiving application entity
- the receiving application entity issues a P-RELEASE response indicating its willingness to accept the termination
- the called presentation entity passes this response to the session service as an S-RELEASE response

- the calling presentation entity receives an S-RELEASE confirm and passes it to the initiating application entity as a P-RELEASE confirm

The User Abort service is used when a communication partner needs to end a connection immediately, the result normally of a severe local error condition. This service is performed using P-U-ABORT primitives which may contain the following parameters:

- presentation context identifier list — used to indicate the context identifers for the contexts used in the user data parameter

- user data — used to pass information from the initiating application entity to the receiver

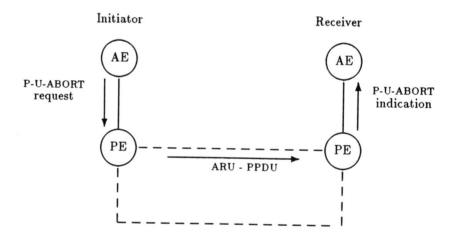

Figure 9.5 User Abort service

User Abort is an unconfirmed service and consists of the following steps (see Figure 9.5):

- the initiating application entity issues a P-U-ABORT request primitive to its PSAP

- the calling presentation entity formats and sends an Abnormal Release User PPDU (ARU-PPDU) to the called presentation entity

- the called presentation entity receives the ARU-PPDU and issues a P-U-ABORT indication to the receiving application entity

The Provider Abort service is used by the Presentation Layer to indicate to the two communication partners that their connection has been lost (in which case the future integrity of the connection could not be guaranteed), due either to receipt of an unexpected PPDU or to receipt of an S-P-ABORT indication from the session service. The presentation service performs a provider abort by passing a P-P-ABORT indication primitive to the application entities, containing the following parameters:

- provider reason — used to inform the application entity of the reason for the termination

- abort data — used to indicate which unexpected PPDU was received by the presentation entity (if this was the reason for termination)

Provider Abort is a provider-initiated service and consists of the following steps (see Figure 9.6):

- a presentation entity receives an S-P-ABORT indication or an unexpected PPDU

- a P-P-ABORT indication is formatted and sent to the connected application entity

Having discussed at length the action of the significant primitives associated with the presentation service, it is unnecessary to deal with the remaining primitives in detail. Figure 9.7 contains an outline of each primitive, its parameters, type of service (C — confirmed, U — unconfirmed, P — provider-initiated) and associated PPDUs.

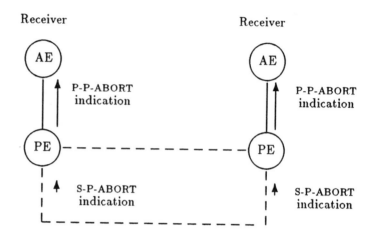

Figure 9.6 Provider Abort service

9.3   Discussion of Technologies

In common with the other upper layers of the OSI model, the development of the Presentation Layer has not been rapid. Work is continuing on such areas as:

- optimisation of operations to reduce the quantity of communicable data that is not representing information

- interrupt processing to allow the presentation operation to be suspended and resumed without the need to terminate the connection

The Presentation Layer is required in open systems where it is necessary to translate between incompatible representations of data. Increasingly, moves towards standardization in areas other than OSI are making this translation function of the layer redundant. The CCITT X.400 recommendations do, however, make provision for a Presentation Layer in X.400 message handling systems.

PRIMITIVE	PARAMETERS	TYPE	PPDUs
P-CONNECT	CALLING PSAP	C	CP
	CALLED PSAP		CPA
	RESPONDING PSAP		CPR
	MULTIPLE CONTEXTS		
	CONTEXT DEF LIST		
	DEFAULT CONTEXT		
	QUALITY OF SERVICE		
	PRESENTATION REQS		
	SESSION REQS		
	INITIAL SYNC NUMBER		
	INITIAL TOKENS		
	SESSION CONNECT ID		
	RESULT		
	USER DATA		
P-DATA	USER DATA	U	TD
P-EXPEDITED-DATA	USER DATA	U	TE
P-TYPED-DATA	USER DATA	U	TTD
P-CAPABILITY-DATA	USER DATA	C	TC
			TCC
P-ALTER-CONTEXT	CONTEXT DEF LIST	C	AC
	CONTEXT DEL LIST		ACA
	USER DATA		
P-TOKEN-PLEASE	TOKEN ITEM	U	
P-TOKEN-GIVE	TOKEN ITEM	U	
P-CONTROL-GIVE	NONE	U	
P-SYNC-MINOR	TYPE	C	
	SYNC NUMBER		
	USER DATA		
P-SYNC-MAJOR	SYNC NUMBER	C	
	USER DATA		
P-RESYNCHRONIZE	TYPE	C	RS
	SYNC NUMBER		RSA
	TOKEN ITEM		
	CONTEXT ID LIST		
	USER DATA		
P-P-EXCEPTION-REPORT	REASON	P	
P-U-EXCEPTION-REPORT	REASON	U	
	USER DATA		
P-ACTIVITY-START	ACTIVITY ID	U	
	USER DATA		
P-ACTIVITY-INTERRUPT	REASON	C	
P-ACTIVITY-RESUME	ACTIVITY ID	U	
	OLD ACTIVITY ID		
	SYNC NUMBER		
	OLD SESSION CONNECT ID		
	USER DATA		
P-ACTIVITY-DISCARD	REASON	C	
P-ACTIVITY-END	SYNC NUMBER	C	
	USER DATA		
P-RELEASE	USER DATA	U	
	RESULT		
P-U-ABORT	USER DATA	U	ARU
	CONTEXT ID LIST		
P-P-ABORT	PROVIDER REASON	P	ARP
	ABORT DATA		

Figure 9.7 Summary of Presentation Layer primitives

9.4   References

9.1 *Open Systems Interconnection: connection-oriented presentation service definition* (DD 101), British Standards Institution, 1986. (This Draft for Development is the equivalent of ISO/DIS 8822.)

9.2 *Open Systems Interconnection: connection-oriented presentation protocol specification* (DD 102), British Standards Institution, 1986. (This Draft for Development is the equivalent of ISO/DIS 8823.)

9.3   *Open Systems Interconnection: specification of Abstract Syntax Notation One (ASN.1)* (DD 103), British Standards Institution, 1985. (This Draft for Development is the equivalent of ISO/DIS 8824.2.)

9.4   *Open Systems Interconnection: specification of basic encoding rules for Abstract Syntax Notation One (ASN.1)* (DD 104), British Standards Institution, 1986. (This Draft for Development is the equivalent of ISO/DIS 8825.2.)

10 Application Layer – Layer 7

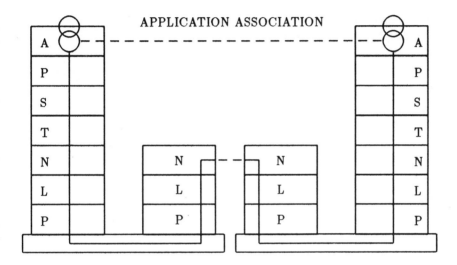

We have now arrived at the highest layer of the OSI model, where the model and the world of application processes meet and interact. This layer is different from all the other layers in that it does not have a strictly defined interface with a higher layer: instead, the Application Layer and application processes overlap. The application process consists of two parts, one which performs processing outside the OSI environment and one which resides within the Application Layer.

A parallel with Application Layer services may be found at an international conference where delegates from many countries meet. The main aim of the conference is to discuss given topics and hopefully to reach some conclusion. However, many of the delegates may only speak their mother tongue, and some may not be able to attend in person, but may use teleconferencing facilities instead. The use of headphones, microphones and interpreters supports communication between the delegates, but has nothing to do with the aims of the conference itself. As far as the delegates are concerned, the ability to communicate is taken for granted and they have no reason to question how it is provided.

The sum of the conferencing services described above is equivalent to the total service of the OSI model. Each of the delegates corresponds with an application carrying out its particular function outside OSI. When communication with other delegates is required, the delegate need only make use of his own communications facilities, his voice and his microphone, as a means of access to the global conferencing facility. In the same way, the Application Layer provides a 'window' into the underlying OSI communications facilities.

In addition to services provided to applications by the Application Layer, there are some global OSI functions for which application protocols will be defined. Such functions already identified include OSI management, security management and directory services.

10.1   Requirements for Layer 7

The main requirement for the Application Layer is that it should provide a window into the OSI environment for application processes which wish to communicate with each other.

Application processes perform many different functions and need to use many different aspects of the OSI environment. The Application Layer is not, therefore, as easily defined in terms of services and protocols as are the other layers. Instead, a number of application types have been identified, corresponding with those general areas of application processing where OSI is particularly relevant — file transfer being an example. Each of these application types has its own requirements and is defined by its own set of standards. Application Layer standards have been produced (or are in the process of production) for the following specific functions within the layer:

- Virtual Terminal services (VT)
- File Transfer, Access and Management (FTAM)
- Job Transfer and Manipulation (JTM)
- transaction processing (TP)

Application Layer standards also exist to cover functions which are common to several different application types. The following are currently defined:

- Association Control (AC)
- Commitment, Concurrency and Recovery (CCR)

Although these functions are described in different, application-oriented standards (for example, Reference 10.1), they need not be used strictly in isolation. The functional Application Layer standards make use of AC and CCR to support their own particular requirements. They may also use other functional standards if necessary to perform a given task; an application entity may make use of JTM to initiate a particular job, and within that job it may use FTAM to transfer files to some other system. CCR will also be used to ensure the correct completion of the job.

10.2   Specification of Layer 7

The Application Layer is different from all other layers in two fundamental areas: it does not provide services to a higher layer and it has no need of a service access point. An application process which wishes to communicate with another application process makes use of an application entity (see Figure 10.1). The application entity consists of a *user element*, which represents the application process which wishes to communicate, and a selection of *application service elements* (ASEs) which provide access to OSI facilities. In order to support communication, the ASEs provide services to the user element. The ASEs support communication with application entities in other open systems by exchanging application protocol data units (APDUs) across a presentation connection.

Some ASEs (sometimes known as *common* application service elements) perform general functions, while others (sometimes known as *specific* application service elements) provide facilities for particular application requirements such as FTAM or JTM. ASEs thus provide groupings of related application services. The two ASEs for general use, the Association Control service element and the Commitment, Concurrency and Recovery service element will be

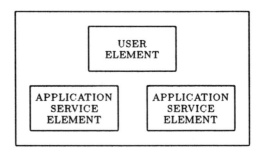

Figure 10.1 Application entity

described, followed by the specific ASEs.

The Association Control service element provides for the creation and release of an association between two application entities. An association is an agreement to exchange information according to a set of limitations known as an *application context*. The application context is a named set of application service elements, options and other information necessary to support the meaningful exchange of data between associated application entities. The name of the required application context is sent as part of the A-ASSOCIATE request; the destination application entity may then either accept the suggested context or propose another. The name returned as part of an A-ASSOCIATE response defines the actual context to be used.

The Association Control service element provides four primitives:

- A-ASSOCIATE
- A-RELEASE
- A-ABORT
- A-P-ABORT

A-ASSOCIATE provides a confirmed service which allows an association to be set up between two application entities. The parameters passed with the A-ASSOCIATE primitive may be grouped into three areas: application parameters, presentation parameters and session parameters.

The application parameters are those which apply to the Application Layer. The parameters for an A-ASSOCIATE request or indication comprise the following:

- called and calling application titles (where an application title is a unique identifier of an application entity)
- application context name
- user information

The parameters for an A-ASSOCIATE response or confirm are as follows:

- responding application title
- result
- application context name
- user information

The A-ASSOCIATE parameters are passed in the P-CONNECT primitive — the application parameters in the user data field and the presentation and session parameters in the corresponding fields (see Figure 10.2). By passing parameters in this way, the application association is set up at the same time as the presentation connection.

A-RELEASE provides a confirmed service which allows the release of a current association. The parameters passed for an A-RELEASE request or indication are as follows:

- release reason
- user data

The parameters passed for an A-RELEASE response or confirm are as follows:

- release reason
- user data
- result

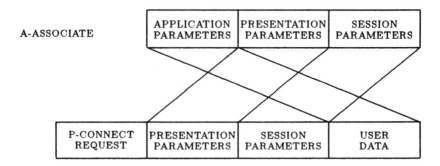

A-ASSOCIATE

P-CONNECT

Figure 10.2 A-ASSOCIATE/P-CONNECT mapping

The A-RELEASE makes use of the P-RELEASE facility, thus releasing the presentation connection at the same time as the application association. The APDU generated by A-RELEASE is passed as user data in the P-RELEASE request.

A-ABORT provides an unconfirmed service which allows an association to be abnormally released by either application entity. This is the equivalent of a P-U-ABORT in the Presentation Layer and results in the release of both the application association and the presentation connection, with the possible loss of data which is in transit at the time of issue.

A-P-ABORT is a provider-initiated indication that an association has been abnormally released due to a problem occurring within the lower layers.

The Commitment, Concurrency and Recovery (CCR) service element provides services to ensure the successful completion of activities spread across open systems. The concept of an *atomic action* is central to the CCR service element and should be explained here. An atomic action consists of a series of operations. These component operations may be carried out in part by several open systems, but either all or none must be carried out. If an error occurs during the execution of an atomic action, that part of the atomic action which failed may be restarted. If the error cannot be corrected, the whole atomic action must be rolled back to its initial state. In other words, an atomic action is only complete when all of its parts have been completed. When all of the component parts of an atomic action are successfully completed, the atomic action is *committed*. The act of commitment for an atomic action removes the possibility of rolling it back. Individual parts of an atomic action may be complete, but until a commit occurs, they may be rolled back or restarted.

The following primitives are provided by the CCR service element:

- C-BEGIN

- C-PREPARE

- C-READY

- C-REFUSE

- C-COMMIT

- C-ROLLBACK

- C-RESTART

C-BEGIN provides an unconfirmed service which initiates an atomic action. The initiator of the atomic action is known as the *superior* and the receiver of the C-BEGIN is known as the *subordinate*. This relationship helps to define the CCR operations which may be carried out by each of the associated application entities. It is possible for an application to be a subordinate across one association and at the same time to be a superior across another association with a different application entity.

C-PREPARE provides an unconfirmed service which allows a superior to indicate to a subordinate that its part of an atomic action is complete, and that it should be prepared to commit.

C-READY provides an unconfirmed service allowing a subordinate to indicate its willingness to commit.

C-REFUSE provides an unconfirmed service allowing a subordinate to refuse to commit its part of an atomic action.

C-COMMIT provides a confirmed service which allows a superior to request commitment of an atomic action. If the subordinate has already indicated its willingness to commit by sending a C-READY, it cannot refuse to commit. Once an atomic action is committed, it cannot be undone or rolled back.

C-ROLLBACK provides a confirmed service which allows a superior to order that an atomic action be rolled back to the state at which the C-BEGIN was issued.

C-RESTART provides a confirmed service allowing an atomic action or part of an atomic action to be restarted from a known point.

By using the primitives shown above, a multi-part, distributed atomic action may be initiated by a single application entity and executed by a number of application entities in different open systems. Wherever it is executed, it must always either be completed or be rolled back to the state before the atomic action was initiated.

The application service elements described so far are of a general nature and may be required irrespective of the particular application type which is making use of the OSI environment. Other application service elements are available which are defined for use in specific application areas. We will discuss each of the areas separately, but there is no actual restriction on their use. As long as the application service elements for each application area are specified in the current application context, they can be used whenever required.

The Virtual Terminal services (VT) support interactive applications where one partner in the interaction is a terminal user. The actual terminal and terminal user are not part of the OSI environment, but the software necessary to drive the terminal may be seen as an OSI application. Terminal support in the OSI environment poses a problem due to the diversity of terminal types and terminal protocols. It is undesirable for an application in one open system to have to provide explicit interfaces for a variety of different terminal types. This would require a large development outlay, and would cause additional work if a new terminal type were added. This problem is solved by the use of a *virtual terminal* (see Figure 10.3).

The virtual terminal is a standard device which is understood by all communicating open systems. A virtual terminal control program manipulates the virtual terminal and communicates all changes made to it using a virtual terminal protocol. Each open system then has a virtual terminal interface which provides access to the virtual terminal. This interface supports an application wishing to communicate with a terminal device. It also supports the terminal drivers for local physical terminals, thus allowing actions carried out on the virtual terminal to be reflected on the physical terminal. An application which drives a terminal actually drives the local virtual terminal, and any changes made to it are detected by the control program and transmitted to the equivalent virtual terminal in the destination system. The destination system detects the changes in its virtual terminal and reflects those changes on the physical terminal by way of a terminal driver process. By using this virtual terminal device, a system only needs to be able to drive its own terminals: terminals in other systems are all accessed using the same interface, regardless of the physical terminal type.

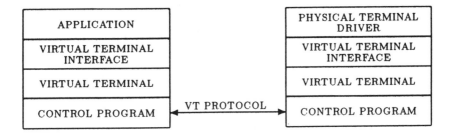

Figure 10.3 Virtual terminal

Work on the Virtual Terminal standards has been continuing over a long period of time. Initially, work was concentrated in two areas: basic class terminals and a generic standard. The basic class terminal is a simple character-oriented terminal; the generic standard encompasses all types of terminal devices including page-oriented terminals and graphics terminals. There were problems with the

definition of the generic standard to such a degree that work on
the basic class was also disrupted. This led to work on the generic
standard being shelved and all efforts being concentrated on the
basic class. The basic class standard is now available along with
some extensions in Draft Addendum (DAD) form. These extensions
make the basic class much more useful by allowing the specification
of *forms* mode, which allows for the display of formatted screens
and for the division of screens into protected and unprotected fields.
Protected fields, which are usually headings, may not be changed;
unprotected fields can accept data input. Screens of this type are
commonplace in modern transaction processing systems.

The following primitives are provided by the Virtual Terminal
service basic class:

- VT-ASSOCIATE — to set up a VT association and to agree
  on the rules governing the association

- VT-RELEASE — to terminate a VT association in an orderly
  way

- VT-U-ABORT — to allow a VT user to terminate an association
  immediately with a possible loss of data

- VT-P-ABORT — to notify VT users of the failure of an
  association

- VT-SWITCH-PROFILE — to change the VT profile governing
  an association

- VT-START-NEG — to allow a negotiated change to the active
  VT environment parameters

- VT-END-NEG — to terminate negotiation

- VT-NEG-INVITE — to invite a peer VT user to propose
  changes to the VT environment parameters

- VT-NEG-OFFER — to offer a set of proposed changes to the
  VT environment parameters

- VT-NEG-ACCEPT — to select a set of new VT environment
  parameters from those offered

- VT-NEG-REJECT — to reject a set of VT environment
  parameters from those offered

- VT-DATA — to update display data on the virtual terminal and to report updates to a peer VT user

- VT-DELIVER — to indicate when a set of VT-DATA updates may be delivered to a peer VT user

- VT-ACK-RECEIPT — to acknowledge receipt of a VT-DELIVER indication

- VT-GIVE-TOKENS — to allow a peer VT user the ownership of the VT access right for synchronous mode operation

- VT-REQUEST-TOKENS — to request the ownership of the VT access right for synchronous mode operation

The File Transfer, Access and Management (FTAM) services allow for file information, both structure and data, to be transferred between open systems. FTAM addresses a similar problem to the Virtual Terminal service in that there are many different implementations of files and file access methods in different systems. The solution in this case is the provision of a *virtual filestore* within each open system with a structure which is known to all open systems (see Figure 10.4). Any file transfer operations which are required are specified in terms of the virtual filestore. The mapping of those operations on to a specific file system is then the responsibility of the controlling open system.

The actions which may be carried out on FTAM files can be divided into two areas: actions on files, performed on the complete file, and actions on data within files. Actions on files include file creation, opening and closing files, reading and changing file attributes and file deletion. Actions on file data include locating, reading, writing and deleting file records.

The FTAM services provide a means to manipulate a virtual filestore according to instructions sent and received using the FTAM protocol. There are five different classes of FTAM service:

- File Transfer class — allows for the bulk transfer of all data in a file

- File Access class — allows access to data within a file

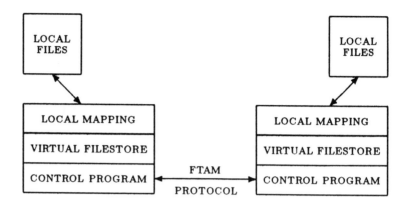

Figure 10.4 Virtual filestore

- File Management class — allows for the access and control of file attributes

- File Transfer and Management class — allows for a combination of file transfer and file management class capabilities

- Unconstrained class — allows for use of any FTAM services and may be used for the implementation of non-standard applications

The smallest part of an FTAM file which may be accessed is a *data unit* (DU), which is equivalent to a record. Accessible units within a file are known as *file access data units* (FADUs) which are arranged in a hierarchical tree structure, each subtree being a FADU. The top level FADU is the whole file (see Figure 10.5).

The following primitives are provided by FTAM to support actions on files:

- F-INITIALIZE — to set up an FTAM association and agree on the services to be used.

- F-TERMINATE — to end an FTAM association in a controlled way

- F-U-ABORT — to allow an application to terminate abnormally an FTAM association

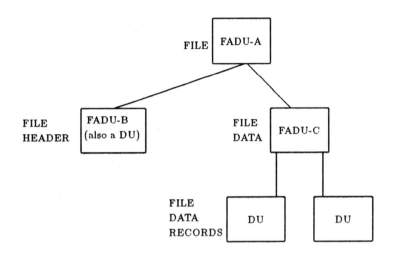

Figure 10.5 FADUs and DUs

- **F-P-ABORT** — to indicate an abnormal termination of an FTAM association initiated by the FTAM service provider

- **F-SELECT** — to identify a file which is to be accessed

- **F-DESELECT** — to release a file which was previously selected

- **F-CREATE** — to create a new file

- **F-DELETE** — to delete an existing file

- **F-READ-ATTRIB** — to obtain details of the attributes of a particular file

- **F-CHANGE-ATTRIB** — to amend the attributes of a file

- **F-OPEN** — to allow access to the contents of a file for read or write access

- **F-CLOSE** — to close a file which has previously been opened

- **F-READ** — to request data from within a file

- **F-WRITE** — to insert data into an open file

- **F-DATA** — to transfer bulk data from or to a file

- F-DATA-END — to indicate the end of a series of F-DATA indications

- F-CHECK — to allow the insertion of a checkpoint in a data transfer

- F-RESTART — to restart a data transfer from a checkpoint

- F-TRANSFER-END — to indicate the end of a series of data transfers

The Job Transfer and Manipulation (JTM) services provide support for a distributed processing environment by allowing an application process in one system to start and monitor jobs in other systems. JTM is not concerned with the actual mechanics of running a particular job, but simply supports the initiation of a job and the transfer of information associated with that job whenever and wherever necessary. The aim of JTM is to provide a complete distribution of job execution such that a job can be initiated by any system, run on any system, accept input and make use of files on any system and provide output to any system. JTM provides control for all of these functions and also provides monitoring and modification of an executing job.

It should be noted that the term 'job' as used within OSI (and particularly in JTM) is not necessarily the equivalent of the term as traditionally applied to, for example, jobs initiated by remote job entry stations. JTM allows for the passage of information (collected into *documents*) to a destination system in order to allow that system to perform its processing. JTM has no interest in the actual processing, and no influence on job control languages (JCL). A traditional job consists of data and instructions to be executed. JTM supports the transportation of the data and instructions, but not the execution.

An OSI job is started by an initiating agency which performs job initiation, thus creating an initial work specification. The work specification contains a definition of the work to be done for a specific job, including information relating to the whole OSI job, the initial subjob, and subsequent subjobs. A subjob is the work necessary to process a single work specification, including starting subsequent subjobs, but not including the work carried out by those subjobs. Information regarding subjobs other than the first is contained within a *proforma* (see Figure 10.6). A proforma contains information which, combined with the OSI job parameters for the whole job, can be used to create a work specification for a subjob. This process is known as *spawning*. It is possible for a proforma to contain further proformas which will in turn be used to create further subjobs. In this way, a single initial work specification can start an infinite chain of jobs.

INITIAL WORK SPECIFICATION

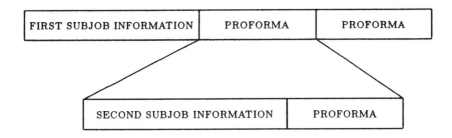

Figure 10.6 Work specification

There are two classes of job transfer:

- Basic class — allows for only one level of proforma in a work specification, thus restricting the spawning of subsequent jobs

- Full class — allows the full set of functions with no limits on proformas in a job specification

JTM is provided by the following set of JTM services:

- J-INITIATE — to start an OSI job

- J-DISPOSE — to deliver documents to a destination agency

- J-GIVE — to receive documents from a source agency

- J-ENQUIRE — to obtain information about documents held by an agency

- J-MESSAGE — to report a message to an OSI job monitor
- J-SPAWN — to create a new work specification from a proforma in an existing work specification
- J-TASKEND — used following a J-DISPOSE to spawn from proformas passed by that J-DISPOSE
- J-STATUS — to obtain information on the status of a link or execution agency
- J-HOLD — to suspend an activity
- J-RELEASE — to cancel a J-HOLD
- J-KILL — to request termination of an activity started by a J-DISPOSE, without providing any output documents
- J-STOP — to request termination of an activity, but allowing output documents to be made available if requested

Transaction processing is becoming a very important mode of working in many systems, but at the time of writing there is no OSI standard to support it. However, work has started on the definition of an OSI transaction processing service (OSI TP) and hopefully a draft standard will become available in the not too distant future.

In addition to the specific application areas mentioned above, the Application Layer is also the location for OSI management functions. OSI management is divided into two areas: *system management* and *layer management*. OSI system management controls OSI resources across all layers. It does this both by means of a system management protocol in the Application Layer and by providing an interface to each layer (see Figure 10.7).

OSI layer management is concerned with management of the resources and activities of each of the individual layers. Data transfers concerned with layer management may take place using the communications facilities provided by that layer although primitives for doing so are not yet included in the layer standard. Alternatively communication may take place via the layer management interface into system management and hence the system management protocol

SYSTEM
MANAGEMENT

SYSTEM
MANAGEMENT

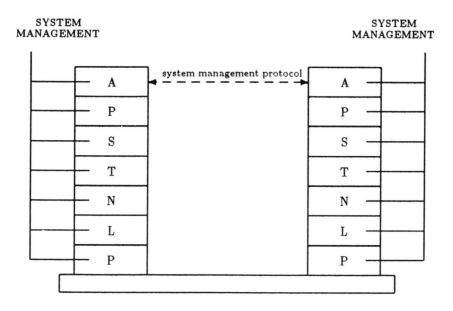

Figure 10.7 System management

at the Application Layer.   OSI management is assisted by the existence of a *management information base* (MIB) which contains all relevant management information for the system in which it resides.

Another management function is the provision of *directory services*.   In order to communicate between open systems, it is first necessary to identify the destination for a data transfer or a connection request — by means of, for example, the destination application title. This is achieved by allocating a unique address for each destination within the OSI network.   Having allocated addresses, a mechanism is now required to select the correct address for an entity with which communication is required. This mechanism is supplied by directory services which will appear as a single global service.   In practice, access to directory services will be via an Application Layer protocol between distributed parts of the directory, each of which will hold information on a part of the open system network known as a *domain*. A fuller discussion of the domain concept may be found in Chapter 6.

The final management function is *security management*.   The

Application Layer has been identified as a potential location for some areas of security, specifically *access control* and *traffic flow security*. In addition to the OSI aspects of security, application processes may also include their own security mechanisms. In common with other management functions, security management makes use of a management information base, known as the *security management information base* (SMIB). The local SMIB may be accessed by any layer in order to obtain security information; in addition to this, it may be required to exchange security management information between open systems. To achieve this, security management protocols will be defined at the Application Layer in the future.

10.3   Discussion of Technologies

Most of the standards which define the Application Layer services are still under development, and some of these are a long way from ratification. Progress should be fairly rapid over the next few years, particularly in the areas of OSI transaction processing, OSI management and OSI directory services. Even where draft standards are already available (for example, FTAM and JTM), further work is still required to produce fully functional standards.

Some products are already available for communications services which are based on the OSI model, but which are not based exclusively on OSI layer standards. Examples of this are the Manufacturing Automation Protocol (MAP) originating from General Motors and the CCITT X.400 message handling system (MHS) group of recommendations which are relevant to the Application and Presentation layers. A more detailed discussion of these areas is presented in Chapter 11.

The general trend for implementation at the Application Layer is the selection of an application protocol (for example, FTAM) and the implementation of only those protocols required at each layer to support that application protocol. This is in effect taking a vertical slice through all seven layers, known as a *functional profile* or *functional standard*. This approach is adopted for two reasons: first, it is easier to develop a specific environment than a general one; secondly, it is cheaper and quicker to implement a specific product using a limited subset of OSI facilities than it is to develop the full set of facilities. Work in this area has been taken up by an organization known as the Standards Promotion and Application Group (SPAG), a group of European information technology suppliers. SPAG is not a formal standards body, but has published a *Guide to the Use of Standards* (GUS) which has had a significant effect on the development of functional profiles in the European context.

10.4 References

10.1 *Open Systems Interconnection: definition of common application service elements: association control* (DD 131), British Standards Institution, 1986. (This Draft for Development is the equivalent of ISO/DIS 8649/2.)

10.2 *Open Systems Interconnection: specification of protocols for application service elements: association control* (DD 132), British Standards Institution, 1986. (This Draft for Development is the equivalent of ISO/DIS 8650/2.)

10.3 *Open Systems Interconnection: definition of common application service elements: commitment, concurrency and recovery* (DD 109), British Standards Institution, 1985. (This Draft for Development is the equivalent of ISO/DIS 8649/3.)

10.4 *Open Systems Interconnection: specification of protocols for common application service elements: commitment, concurrency and recovery* (DD 110), British Standards Institution, 1985. (This Draft for Development is the equivalent of ISO/DIS 8650/3.)

10.5 *Open Systems Interconnection: job transfer and manipulation concepts and services* (DD 105), British Standards Institution, 1985. (This Draft for Development is the equivalent of ISO/DP 8831.)

10.6   *Open Systems Interconnection: specification of the basic class protocol for job transfer and manipulation* (DD 106), British Standards Institution, 1985. (This Draft for Development is the equivalent of ISO/DP 8832.)

10.7   *Open Systems Interconnection: file transfer, access and management* (DD 113, parts 1 to 4), British Standards Institution, 1985. (This Draft for Development is the equivalent of ISO/DP 8571/1 – 4.)

10.8   *Open Systems Interconnection: virtual terminal services: basic class* (DD 129), British Standards Institution, 1986. (This Draft for Development is the equivalent of ISO/DIS 9040.)

10.9   *Open Systems Interconnection: virtual terminal protocol: basic class* (DD 130), British Standards Institution, 1986. (This Draft for Development is the equivalent of ISO/DIS 9041.)

10.10   *Open Systems Interconnection: security architecture* (DD 148), British Standards Institution, 1986. (This Draft for Development is the equivalent of ISO 7498/PDAD 2.)

11 Applications of OSI

The reader who has come this far might be forgiven for thinking that for so powerful and flexible a concept as OSI, its universal application can only be a matter of time. The unremitting and sometimes misleading publicity which OSI has received in the computer trade press over recent years has tended to purvey an image of a universal solution to all problems of data communications and system incompatibility. However, like all technologies it has strengths and weaknesses which limit the range of problems to which it can be successfully applied. The purpose of this chapter is to identify these limitations, and also describe some of the successful applications which are already being realised.

The limitations of OSI stem from three sources:

- the technical constraints imposed by the layered structure
- some facilities essential for practical communications are not yet specified by OSI standards
- the political limitations arising from its genesis as a set of non-proprietary protocols, devised by international agreement

11.1 Technical Limitations

The most obvious difficulty in the practical use of OSI is its complexity. When first conceived, the seven layer model represented a greater decomposition of the problem of data communications than previously considered necessary; most proprietary protocol 'stacks' make do with four layers. Within each OSI layer options abound, such as the five classes of transport protocol, and the functional subsets in the Session Layer. The result is enormous complexity in specification and implementation, which leads to software that is less reliable, less efficient, and more costly. Typical current experience is that the OSI transport protocol gives 30 per cent less throughput for a given level of processor resources than the comparable native proprietary protocol. However, it is generally recognised that as OSI software is progressively refined this difference will become less significant.

A more important consequence of the complexity of OSI standards is the difficulty of ensuring that they are unambiguous and correct as published. The standards are currently expressed as natural language clauses, with state tables and diagrams to show state transitions. Inevitably there are ambiguities which find their way into real implementations. To overcome this problem there is a move towards more formal methods of specification in the OSI community, using Abstract Syntax Notation One (ASN.1) and definition languages such as Estelle and LOTOS.

The other major technical limitation of OSI is that it is inherently connection-oriented. This can be seen in nearly all of the layer specifications, in the division of protocols into connection establishment, data transfer and connection release phases. This has consequences in two respects:

- certain applications are inherently connectionless, and OSI is unable to support them efficiently, if at all

- some communications technologies are connectionless in concept, such as the CSMA/CD and Token Ring standards for local area networks. Successful operation of Layers 5 to 7 over a path which is connectionless at Layer 2 demands a careful selection of compatible options from Layers 2, 3 and 4

An example of a connectionless application is the distribution of radar track data for air traffic control or within a ship. Each track message is quite short, consisting of the position, identification, and velocity of a track, and a timestamp. It is sent to multiple destinations, such as operator screens and navigation systems. Since each track is updated on every sweep of the radar antenna, an individual track message is only valid for a few seconds, and if it does not reach its destination in that time it may as well be discarded. Setting up and breaking down an OSI connection for every message and source/destination pair would be impossible. Maintaining a set of continuously-open connections from the radar to the receiving devices is a more plausible approach, but it would be very inefficient due to the small amount of data in each message, which must be transmitted immediately because of its perishability. In practice a 'datagram' mode is used, where each track message is packaged with sufficient address and error control data to be a self-contained communication.

The problem of including a connectionless Layer 2 in an OSI network is an important one, since most practical networks will have a local area network as part of the physical communications provision. Often the LAN must interconnect with a connection-oriented wide area network such as the public X.25 network. Essentially there are two possible approaches, depending on whether a connection-oriented or connectionless Network Layer is implemented. In the first case a Class 1 or Class 2 transport protocol is indicated, combined with a selection of Layer 2 protocols providing error recovery and flow control. In the second case a Class 4 transport protocol is required, giving error recovery and flow control, which may be combined with simple non-error correcting Layer 2 protocols such as LLC Type 1.

11.2 Limitations by Omission

The most important omission from the current set of standards and drafts is network management. The topic is being addressed in OSI working groups, using the concept of a management information base (see Chapter 10) which is available to communicating open systems. A comprehensive set of management functions is envisaged, including:

- fault management
- accounting management
- configuration management
- performance management
- security management
- directory services

At the time of writing this book a *management framework* has been defined, but individual management topics are less well advanced. All are essential to any large scale network; current implementations use proprietary or *ad hoc* software to provide these facilities.

A common use of data communications is transaction processing, where a user updates or inspects a remote database by filling in forms displayed at a terminal. No OSI standard supports this activity at the Application Layer, although clearly the lower layer standards could be used to convey transaction messages. The Virtual Terminal standards which are under development will be helpful in respect of screen handling aspects. A draft proposal, published in 1985, for a connection-oriented transaction processing standard derived from the IBM SNA LU6.2 protocol, was not adopted. Currently a more European approach is being pursued which is connectionless and employs a 'remote procedure call' mechanism.

A practical problem in integrating OSI products from several vendors is the lack of standards for parameters such as the maximum number of concurrent connections, maximum message length, and timeouts following a failure before recovery action is initiated. Effectively these must be agreed on by the community within which an open system operates, and all OSI products used must be capable of being configured consistently.

11.3   Political Limitations

The success of OSI is seen by the major governments of the EEC as vital to the survival and prosperity of their domestic computer manufacturers. As a result 'support for OSI' is being written into a wide range of public sector invitations to tender. This has placed manufacturers under pressure to offer OSI products as soon as possible in order to show their commitment. In practice these products are often early releases with little operational experience behind them. The many options within OSI tend to be incompletely implemented, and these gaps may be glossed over in the documentation in the hope that the high cost of the software will encourage users to adopt a proprietary solution.

In order to sustain confidence amongst users, the practice of 'third party' testing has been introduced. In the UK, the National Computing Centre and British Telecom are equipped to offer OSI conformance testing services. Suppliers of OSI software can offer their products to these test houses for an independent evaluation against a series of tests, which check for the existence of a minimum set of facilities (static conformance) and correct state machine behaviour in operation (dynamic conformance). The design of these tests is itself undergoing a process of international harmonization to ensure that testing does at least increase the probability that independently-produced products can communicate. Because testing cannot be exhaustive, it is no guarantee of 'first-time' success.

Meanwhile the development of proprietary network products, particularly DECnet and SNA, proceeds apace. Both will tend at any time to offer more facilities at a lower cost than OSI. The system developer will therefore always have to weigh the benefit of vendor independence against the higher cost and technical risk of an OSI solution. Some important application areas where this equation comes out in favour of OSI are discussed in the next section.

11.4   Natural Applications of OSI

The key attribute of OSI is vendor independence, and when this consideration is paramount, OSI becomes the natural solution. When an application demands coordination between a number of independent organizations, it is likely that each will have its own hardware preferences and loyalties, and OSI becomes the common denominator on which all can agree. This is particularly true where the organizations have a peer group (that is, non-hierarchical) relationship, and even more so when they are competitors in a particular industry sector. In the latter case, to adopt a vendor-specific solution would give a competitive advantage to the vendor's clients in the industry and hence could not be contemplated.

Examples of such 'communities of interest' which are working towards the construction of OSI networks include:

- universities — the Joint Network Team which manages the UK universities network is in the process of changing from the 'Coloured Book' protocols, which have provided vendor-independent data communications for many years, to OSI standards

- aircraft industry — AECMA, the association of European

aerospace manufacturers, has a working group to promote the exchange of design and manufacturing information between companies engaged on cooperative projects such as Airbus and Tornado

- motor industry — the ODETTE initiative is being sponsored by the EEC to standardize the exchange of commercial documents such as invoices and quotations for car components. General Motors has also promoted the MAP manufacturing standards, which are examined in detail below

- banking — an ISO working group is engaged on the application of OSI to inter-bank communications. SWIFT II, a new version of the existing inter-bank network, is defined in OSI terms and will use OSI protocols as they become commercially available

For these community of interest networks to be successful, an additional form of standardization is required in conjunction with OSI standards. Each community has a number of real world objects of interest to it, such as bank balances, car parts and aircraft design drawings. The community aiming for standardization must agree on the representation of these objects as data items, typically by constructing a data dictionary whose definitions will be used on new information technology projects within the community. These data items may then be assembled into agreed message or record formats and exchanged using the Application Layer utilities provided by OSI, such as FTAM or VT.

Having determined the semantics and syntax of data exchange — the 'language' of the community — the mechanics of OSI must be tidied up by making a selection from the options available at every level. Such a selection becomes a functional standard, as discussed in Chapter 10; by defining how the standards will be interpreted and combined within a 'domain of application', their practical utility is greatly enhanced.

A good example of a set of OSI functional standards combined with a community of interest format standard is MAP. This was devised by General Motors to allow the various automated manufacturing systems on a production line to communicate. Data can then flow in parallel with the products being produced, eliminating 'islands of automation' which otherwise have to be bridged by manual

Layer 7   OSI CASE (ISO 8649, ISO 8650)
               OSI FTAM (ISO 8571)
               EIA RS-511/CCITT X.409
               MAP-specific network management and directory service

Layer 6   OSI Presentation (ISO 8823)

Layer 5   OSI Session (ISO 8327)

Layer 4   OSI Transport Class 4 (ISO 8073)

Layer 3   OSI connectionless Network (ISO 8473)

Layer 2   IEEE 802.2 LLC Types 1 and 3 (ISO 8802/2)
               IEEE 802.4 Token Bus (ISO 8802/4)
               ISA Proway Extensions

Layer 1   IEEE 802.4 Broadband at 10Mb/s
                  or Carrierband at 5Mb/s (ISO 8802/4)

Figure 11.1 MAP 3.0 protocol stack

data entry or transfer of machine-readable media.

     MAP has evolved through a number of releases; the protocol 'stack' for the fifth release (MAP 3.0) is shown in Figure 11.1. Layers 1 and 2 of MAP use the Token Bus local area network standard because of its deterministic propagation delay time which is essential for machine control. Broadband signalling is employed to give greater resistance to electrical noise than a baseband technique, and compatibility with large-scale multi-application factory site networks. The carrierband option is a lower cost version of IEEE 802.4 suitable for short distance networks. The ISA (Instrument Society of America) Proway Extensions consist of extra protocol options added to IEEE 802.4 to speed up time-critical data transfers.

     Layers 3 to 6 represent a straightforward use of OSI, the Session and Presentation Layers being limited to simple kernels. One MAP option, known as Mini-MAP, by-passes these layers altogether for localised, throughput-critical networks. This is achieved by operating the EIA RS-511 format over LLC Type 3 (acknowledged connectionless) at Layer 2. LLC Type 3 incorporates error and flow control, hence the Transport Layer is not essential, and a highly efficient data transfer mechanism is achieved, suitable for low cost or high bit rate applications.

The key standard at Layer 7 is EIA RS-511, which provides a syntax for manufacturing-oriented messages. It makes use of X.409 encoding rules. A set of associated semantic standards is being developed to cover the range of manufacturing contexts, from chemical process control to robotised mechanical assembly.

The discussion above has shown how the vendor independence of OSI leads to its adoption for specialised community of interest applications such as MAP. Vendor independence is also vital to universal forms of communication which are relevant to most businesses or organizations. The best example of such a global application of OSI is X.400, which provides the topic for the following section.

11.5   X.400 Message Handling Systems

More implementations exist of X.400 than of any other Application Layer utility, and practical, economic use of X.400 is becoming commonplace. This has arisen because, rather as in the case of X.25, the CCITT took an early lead in establishing standards based wholly on OSI concepts. Subsequent OSI standards under development will generalize but not supersede X.400.

X.400 exists as a series of CCITT recommendations (numbered from X.400 onwards — Reference 11.1) devised to provide facilities for electronic mail. This may be defined as the distribution of messages prepared by, and intended for interpretation by people rather than computers. Because person-to-person communication is of global interest, as exemplified by the telex and telephone networks, X.400 has received widespread acceptance. X.400 therefore is currently unique in transcending the community of interest boundaries of other OSI applications.

The person-to-person definition may be extended in practice to include users which are computer programs but it serves as an introduction to the structure of X.400. This is based on two Application Layer functional modules: the *user agent* and the *message transfer agent*. These relate to the user and to each other as shown in Figure 11.2.

The user agent as a minimum is able to submit and receive formatted messages in accordance with procedures defined in X.411. Typically, it will provide editing facilities for message preparation and a 'mailbox' for storing incoming messages. The message transfer agent performs a function analogous to the traditional telex message switch, in routeing the formatted message to one or more destination user agents. A set of connected message transfer agents and the parts of attached user agents performing standardized X.400 services form a message handling system (MHS). The MHS model permits message handling systems to be implemented as public or private networks, or combinations of both.

As well as specifying mechanisms for message transmission, X.400 provides some guidance (in X.409) for the content of the message. It enables message format standards to be devised for a particular application context by classifying the required data items into item type (for example, Boolean, integer or text string) and then using a standard notation to represent the data item and any value taken by it. EIA RS-511, the MAP 3.0 message format standard, uses the X.409 notation.

In X.408 the scope for conversion within an X.400 MHS between various forms of information encoding is considered. The options listed vary from the fairly simple (telex to teletex) through quite complex but feasible (telex to facsimile) to more 'way out' possibilities such as voice to videotex. Few of the options are specified but a framework has been constructed for future development which will be of great value to 'office automation' applications of X.400.

X.408 and X.409, by providing data conversion rules and a data transfer syntax, effectively contain the key functions of the Presentation Layer. X.400 implementations therefore usually contain a minimal 'kernel' Presentation Layer or may interface directly to the Session Layer. X.410 specifies the functional units of the Session Layer which are exploited by X.400.

X.410 deals with the various functions of the user agent, including the representation of documents as messages, and the variety of forms of delivery, such as multi-addressing and receipted delivery, that are well understood for physical mail and need to have some electronic parallel. Finally, X.420 specifies protocols for interfacing a teletex

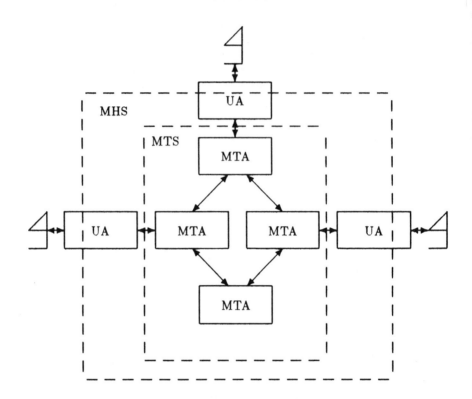

MHS — MESSAGE HANDLING SYSTEM
MTA — MESSAGE TRANSFER AGENT
MTS — MESSAGE TRANSFER SYSTEM
UA — USER AGENT

Figure 11.2 The X.400 message handling system model

terminal to an X.400 MHS.

As ever with complex standards, it has proved necessary for bodies such as SPAG to define functional standards, which encapsulate a subset of options and clarify ambiguities, for practical use. However, it is clearly desirable that the essential principles of X.400 should become as ubiquitous and well-understood as telex.

In summary, X.400 is a versatile set of protocols whose uses go well beyond person-to-person electronic mail. Program-to-program data transfers are just as possible, as long as the data can be packaged into self-contained messages and there are no critical propagation time constraints or requirements for synchronization between messages. Because user agents are usually designed to handle 'dumb' terminals, they can provide a window into OSI for the most rudimentary equipment.

11.6 The Future of OSI

That OSI has a future there can be little doubt, because the enormous effort which has gone into the most complex international standardization initiative in history is finally bearing fruit. Cost-effective, practical OSI applications are being created, based, for example, on portable layer products written in C for UNIX systems. Yet for every draft proposal that finally turns into an international standard, two more seem to be initiated and new working groups created. The solution to this proliferation problem will come through the use of functional standards such as MAP which provide a path for the system builder in each industrial or commercial sector. Where these communities of interest touch, they will communicate using a few globally applicable OSI mechanisms such as X.400.

The vision that computers should be able to communicate as readily as human beings is one which will continue to motivate the evolution of OSI. Software engineering techniques are being developed to meet the technical challenges posed by OSI's complexity; equally, the political and economic challenge to OSI from proprietary solutions has been largely overcome, with all major computer manufacturers planning to offer OSI products. During the next decade and beyond, there is every prospect that OSI will become a cornerstone of information technology.

11.7   Reference

11.1 'Data communication networks: message handling systems. Recommendations X.400 – X.430', *Red Book*, Volume VIII, Fascicle VIII.7, International Telegraph and Telephone Consultative Committee, 1985.

Definition of OSI Terms

Address : The identifier of a **service access point**. Also known as a *service access point address*.

Association : The relationship between two (N)-entities formed when an (N–1)-connection is established between them.

Blocking : The combining of multiple **service data units** with added **protocol control information** into one **protocol data unit**.

Concatenation : The combining of multiple **protocol data units** into one **service data unit** for the layer below.

Connection : A relationship established by the (N)-Layer between two (N+1)-entities for the transfer of data.

Connection endpoint : The end of a connection within a **service access point**. Used to support multiple connections in one service access point.

Connectionless/connection-oriented : Two different modes of communication between systems. Connection-oriented means that a logical connection is first established between the communicating systems to enable the data to be transferred. Connectionless means that a single message, containing routeing information, is passed without first establishing a connection.

Entity : An active element within the (N)-Layer which communicates with a peer element by making use of the services provided by the (N–1)-Layer.

Expedited data transfer : The transfer of data between peer entities with priority over data being transferred normally.

Flow control : A function to control the flow of data between peer entities or between layers such that the receiving entity can limit the rate at which data is transmitted by the sending entity.

Interconnection : A relationship between open systems allowing them to communicate and interwork.

Interface : The boundary between two adjacent layers.

Interface control information (ICI) : Information passed across an **interface** to coordinate interactions between two adjacent layers.

Layer : A subdivision of the OSI architecture. The (N)-Layer provides **services** to the (N+1)-Layer and makes use of services provided by the (N−1)-Layer.

Multiplexing : An (N)-Layer function where a single (N−1)-connection is used to support multiple (N)-connections. *Demultiplexing* restores the multiple (N)-connections.

Primitive : A means of identifying an elementary function provided as part of a layer **service**. Primitives are used either by the (N)-Layer to select a particular service from the (N−1)-Layer, or by the (N−1)-Layer to indicate that a service has been selected.

Protocol : A set of rules governing the format and sequence of information exchanged between communicating peer entities.

Protocol control information (PCI) : Information exchanged between communicating peer entities to coordinate their operation.

Protocol data unit (PDU) : A unit of data specified in a **protocol** and consisting of **protocol control information** and optionally a **user data** field.

Quality of service (QOS) : A description of the set of required operating characteristics provided to an (N)-entity by the (N–1)-service. Usually applies to a particular connection and is negotiated and agreed upon at the time of establishing the connection.

Relay : An intermediate open system with only the lower three layers implemented, used to interconnect end open systems.

Service : A facility which a layer provides to the layer above. The total set of all facilities provided by the (N)-Layer is known as the (N)-service.

Service access point (SAP) : The point of interaction between entities in adjacent layers.

Service data unit (SDU) : A unit of data which is transferred from one end of a connection to the other with no loss of identity or meaning.

Splitting : An (N)-Layer function where multiple (N–1)-connections are used to support a single (N)-connection. *Recombining* restores the single (N)-connection.

Standards Promotion and Application Group (SPAG) : A group representing European companies with an interest in OSI, set up to consider implementation issues of OSI.

Subnetwork : The OSI representation of a real communications network excluding the end open systems.

System : A set of hardware, software, processes, human operators and all other functions required to form an autonomous unit capable of performing information processing.

User data (UD) : Data passed between (N)-entities on behalf of (N+1)-entities. For example, an (N)-SDU will form user data for the (N)-PDU.

Glossary

Architecture : The overall structure of a system and the set of rules governing the interactions between parts of that system.

Circuit-switching : A means of interconnecting multiple end-user systems by the switching of physical connections.

Data terminal equipment (DTE) : A real end system whose network entity has no routeing or relaying functions.

Data circuit-terminating equipment (DCE) : An intermediate system whose network entity has only a routeing and relaying function.

Frame : A delimited stream of data bits transferred at the data link level.

HDLC (High-level data link control) : A set of procedures defining the exchange of data at the data link level.

LAN (local area network) : A network linking computer systems and workstations within a limited geographical area, usually using private physical connections.

Packet : The meaning of packet varies depending on the context in which it is used. In **packet-switching** terms, it is a unit of data transferred through a network. In **X.25** terms, it is a unit of data with a predefined format which is transferred at the packet level of X.25.

Packet-switching : A technique for routeing data through a network in discrete blocks (or **packets**) thus maximising the use of physical connections. The physical connections within the network are shared, with data for different sources and destinations being interleaved.

Routeing : The means of transferring data from a source to a destination identified by its address. It is not necessary for a source system to have knowledge of the intermediate systems used, but it is necessary for intermediate systems to know the correct 'direction' for each destination system.

Transparent data transfer : The transfer of data between systems such that data can be sent in any format, and the received data will be identical to that sent.

Virtual circuit : A logical path through a network between a source system and a destination system. The two communicating systems appear to have exclusive use of a connection, but a dedicated physical link is not provided. Virtual circuits may be switched (SVC) or permanent (PVC).

X.21 : CCITT recommendation for a general purpose interface between **DTE** and **DCE** for synchronous operation on public data networks. (X.21 bis provides the same service for networks using the V Series modems.)

X.25 : CCITT recommendation for the interface between **DTE** and **DCE** for terminals operating in the packet mode.

X.400 : CCITT recommendations for message handling systems.

WAN (wide area network) : A network linking computer systems over a geographically widespread area using both public and private communication connections.

Index

abstract syntax, *see* syntax

Abstract Syntax Notation One (ASN.1), *see* syntax

AC, *see* application service elements

addressing
  see also routeing
  across OSI networks, 93, 97–9, 195
  between layers of OSI model, 37–8
  domain, 98–9, 195
  in Network Layer, 93, 97–9

application, 30–1
  association, 35, 182–4
  context, 182, 186
  entity, 34–6, 160, 181–3, 185–6
  process, 34, 115, 179–81
  protocol data unit (APDU), 181
  service element (ASE), 181–2
  title, 183, 195

Application Layer, 36, 179–98
  function of, 179–80
  implementation of, 196–7
  requirements for, 180–1
  specification of, 181–96

application service elements (ASEs)
  Association Control (AC), 181–4
  Commitment, Concurrency and Recovery (CCR), 181, 184–6
  File Transfer, Access and Management (FTAM), 180–1, 189–92, 196, 204
  Job Transfer and Manipulation (JTM), 180–1, 192–4, 196
  transaction processing (TP), 180, 194, 196
  Virtual Terminal services (VT), 180, 186–9, 202, 204

ARPANET, 9, 10

architecture
  layered, 9–11, 13–25, 29

ASN.1, *see* syntax

association, 35

Association Control (AC), *see* application service elements

asynchronous transmission, *see* data transmission

atomic action, 184–6

Basic Encoding Rules (BER), 163–5

'black box' approach
  to system design, 14

blocking, 41

British Standards Institution (BSI), 6, 26–7

carrier sense, *see* CSMA/CD

CCITT (International Telegraph and Telephone Consultative Committee), 6, 9, 26–7, 98, 206
  see also V Series, X.21, X.25, X.400

CCR, *see* application service elements

circuit
  packet-switched, 9, 91–2, 109
  virtual, 20, 93

circuit-switching, 2–3, 7, 20, 91–2